ABC $ 750

D0758951

SECRET NAVAL INVESTIGATOR

SECRET NAVAL INVESTIGATOR

The Battle Against Hitler's Secret Underwater Weapons

Commander F. Ashe Lincoln QC, RNVR

Preface by Commander Del McKnight RN

FRONTLINE BOOKS

SECRET NAVAL INVESTIGATOR
The Battle Against Hitler's Secret Underwater Weapons

This edition published in 2017 by Frontline Books,
an imprint of Pen & Sword Books Ltd,
47 Church Street, Barnsley, S. Yorkshire, S70 2AS

First published by William Kimber & Co. Limited, London, 1961.

Copyright © Commander F. Ashe Lincoln QC, RNVR.
Preface copyright © Commander Del McKnight RN

The right of Commander F. Ashe Lincoln QC, RNVR to be identified as the
author of this work has been asserted by him in accordance with the
Copyright, Designs and Patents Act 1988.

ISBN: 978-1-52670-119-0

All rights reserved. No part of this publication may be reproduced, stored
in or introduced into a retrieval system, or transmitted, in any form, or by
any means (electronic, mechanical, photocopying, recording or otherwise)
without the prior written permission of the publisher. Any person who
does any unauthorized act in relation to this publication may be liable to
criminal prosecution and civil claims for damages.

CIP data records for this title are available from the British Library

For more information on our books, please visit
www.frontline-books.com
email info@frontline-books.com
or write to us at the above address.

Printed and bound by CPI Group (UK) Ltd, Croydon, CR0 4YY
Typeset in 10.5/12.5 point Palatino

Contents

Preface

When I was originally asked if I would pen a few words of introduction to the book you now hold in your hands, I was both flattered and surprised. As the Commanding Officer of the Royal Navy's Fleet Diving Squadron, it is true I do lead the elite units which, often at high readiness, provide everything from support to special operations, mine countermeasures, bomb disposal on land and at sea and underwater engineering. However, there are many individuals more closely involved in the fight today than I.

It seemed to me, initially at least, that we are a far cry from our predecessors; the heroic men and women who fought for the very survival of our nation during the dark days of the early 1940s. On reading the book, however, I discovered many more parallels than I had expected to find. Like Commander Ashe, we have struggled, in recent years, with ingenious individuals and organisations who have tried to invent ever more intricate ways to defeat our explosive ordnance disposal techniques.

In Northern Ireland, Afghanistan and across the Middle East, to name but a few of the places naval personnel have had to deploy, often far from the sea, we have had to use our wits and intelligence to defeat the cunning of the bomb-maker. In addition, my teams have deployed to clear many of the sea mines off Iraq and the Falklands that would have been familiar to the people in this book. Indeed, even today, my units in the

UK are often called upon to deal with the type of historic bombs and mines described in the following pages.

As a history enthusiast, and someone who strongly believes in the need to study the past to avoid mistakes in the future, I have read many similar accounts of conflicts. This is not a dry tome, however, to be studied only by academics and those who wish to bolster their thesis. It is an entertaining and often witty read which sheds light on many of the very human aspects of the war in Europe between 1939 and 1945. It shows the very real worries and concerns of the brave individuals who used their skills and intelligence to defeat the cutting-edge technology of the time that, had it succeeded, might have cut off the flow of men and material so essential to the ultimate victory. The ground mines of the time incorporated both extremely inventive methods of actuation but also booby traps aimed at defeating the EOD expert and ensuring the mines' secrets remained just that, secret. Had we not worked out how to defeat these weapons it would have led to debilitating losses of merchant vessels supplying the very life blood of the nation, as well as ceding control of the oceans.

In addition, Commander Ashe's work in facilitating the Allied armies' crossing of the Rhine, and the protection of the supply lines from attack to ensure the flow of ammunition and reinforcements, was essential.

Who would have thought that Royal Navy personnel would have been employed deep in the heart of Europe, miles from any sea, in a vital role to bring about the defeat of Germany?

I recommend the book wholeheartedly. It is, perhaps, more of a string of highly entertaining anecdotes such as might be heard hear from a grandfather in front of the fire on a cold winter night, than a detailed rendition full of important but dull detail. Tales such as my own grandfather would never have related, no matter how hard he was pressed, due in the main to his modesty and the belief that he was 'only doing his job' and that others contributed much more. Commander

Ashe, however, did make a huge difference. What is more, by writing this book he brings to life the struggles of the time, making the concerns of the people described in these pages very real and comprehensible.

Commander Del McKnight RN,
CO Fleet Diving Squadron,
Portsmouth, February 2017.

Introduction

I deliberately postponed writing this book until many years had elapsed after the events of the war because of the necessarily secret and confidential nature of the matters with which it deals; but as the years have gone on many books have been published about certain aspects of the work, particularly mine disposal, and it is now quite apparent that very few of the matters concerned can now be considered as highly secret. I decided to write the book now because it would be, in my opinion, a great pity if the work of such a body as "DTMI" (Department of Torpedoes and Mines Investigation Section) remained unknown to the general public. I find that even today the majority of the public do not appreciate that wars are won as much by brainwork and the application of brains as they are by courage and strategy. In my humble opinion great credit is due to the Royal Navy for the way in which it recognised the need for such "back-room" organisations as DTMI, and was prepared to fit them in to the already well-organised pattern of the Service. Undoubtedly there are in every Service some whose attitude and whole psychology is hide-bound by regulation and the existing pattern, but when war comes, important as tradition is, it must sometimes be sacrificed to the needs of the moment. The ability to improvise has always been an outstanding virtue of the British and is exemplified by the account of events which I give in this book.

The story as I set it out is necessarily an incomplete one. The choice had to be made of the more outstanding events and therefore a number of interesting, though possibly minor, aspects of the work had to be omitted. I would like to make two things clear: first and foremost, the work of DTMI was a team-job under the overall direction of Captain A. Maitland-Dougall, R.N., and I have tried to avoid making it appear in this book that it was in any way otherwise. Up to the time of the formation of DTMI the work was done, as I have indicated, by myself working under the command of Admiral Wake-Walker and Captain Denis Boyd (as he then was). From the moment of the formation of DTMI nothing could have been accomplished without the patience and wisdom of Captain Maitland-Dougall to whom I can never in words give adequate praise. I am sure that there were many times when he felt a great impatience at having to be kept more or less solidly at his desk, when in spirit he would much rather have been with the man who was working somewhere on a lonely beach on a new type of weapon. But he clearly recognised that his job was to stay there and direct matters, and to apply the vast store of knowledge which he had accumulated about underwater weapons in his long career as a Torpedo Officer of the Royal Navy.

Of course, both the Captain and myself as his Number One, depended a great deal upon those officers who at various times formed our staff. I have mentioned some of them by name in connection with particular exploits, but all of them showed courage and initiative when called upon. They were willing, at a moment's notice, to dash off to tackle some unknown weapon or investigate some curious and unexplained explosion, but in between jobs of that kind they had to contend with the routine job of assisting us to assess the meaning of events on the basis of reports. We could not have been served by a better or more loyal body of officers than those with whom we had the good fortune to serve in DTMI.

Secondly, I must in advance crave indulgence from any who read this book and who have knowledge of the events therein, for any mistakes which may appear which are due entirely to the lapse of time and fading memories. I have done my best to reconstruct these events from such scrappy notes as I retained, and from checking with others dates, times and places, but with the best will in the world I recognise that mistakes may still have been made. However, I am sure that taken as a whole the story here recounted gives a fair picture of the work of investigation that we achieved.

There were, of course, many sides to this work of investigation, some of them incidents not without humour. For example, there were many occasions when urgent reports were received at the Admiralty to the effect that a new and dangerous-looking object had been washed ashore upon some remote beach, and upon investigation and a gingerly approach by the officer concerned, it turned out to be a log of wood. On another occasion curious objects were reported as floating in the Channel "believed to be enemy explosive devices" which the ships' captains reported as being so cleverly camouflaged that they could not be seen until the ship had almost run them down. These objects turned out to be special kinds of marker devices which had been designed by the Royal Air Force, and according to their experts had been painted in such distinctive colours that they would show up against the normal sea background.

There was also the occasion related to the discovery and rendering safe of the BM 1000 when, in the midst of the chaos caused by the heavy destruction of the raids on the Clyde, it was essential to get additional assistance at short notice because the buildings in the vicinity of the unexploded mines were on fire and there were so many unexploded objects to be dealt with. I managed to find a public telephone box which was still connected to the exchange. I dialled through to the operator and asked to be put through urgently to the Naval Headquarters.

"You must put twopence in the box," she replied.

I protested that I had not in fact the requisite change with me and that this was a matter of the utmost urgency and again requested the call – to be informed that "If ye no ha' twopence ye canna ha' the call!"

I have mentioned the unknown objects which were identified as Royal Air Force markers, and would like to take the opportunity of emphasising how very much we were indebted to the various sections of R.A.F. Intelligence, especially to Squadron Leader Felkin who was one of the Interrogators, and to Squadron Leader Robin Steele of AI2G which was concerned with enemy weapon investigation on behalf of the R.A.F. in much the same way as we were in the Navy. There was a constant interchange of information between these officers and ourselves, and very often mutual discussions of problems and their knowledge and experiences were freely given to us and proved of the greatest benefit. Our relations with Army Intelligence were equally good, and sometimes enabled us to get very valuable advance information.

It may seem to the ordinary reader that co-operation between the Services and, for that matter, between Allies as well, is to be taken for granted, but such is not the case. Co-operation between the Services has always depended, and probably always will depend, on the character and nature of the officers who are called upon to work together. Pride in one's own Service is a very worthy characteristic, but jealousy as to which Service gets the credit for a particular job seems to me to be utterly stupid. Thus I remember in the early days of the war a young R.A.F. officer trying to argue with me that by the end of the war the R.A.F. would be "the Senior Service". I put a speedy end to this discussion by saying that I felt that I really would not care particularly so long as the war was won and we all worked harmoniously together to achieve that end.

I do not think that it is worth while embarking upon the question of co-operation between Allies because quite obviously history places together as Allies on some occasions nations which shortly after are at arm's length; but it is an indication of the greatness of Winston Churchill that his directive to us during the war was always to encourage the widest possible co-operation and the giving of information to all our Allies however meanly they might behave towards us. Churchill would not allow the pettiness of a tit-for-tat attitude and in this I think he has been proved right.

When I was first recalled from sea to work on investigations at the Admiralty I received the news with considerable misgiving. After all I had joined the Navy and trained for it in order to fight at sea, and I was always heartily glad that there was not a legal branch in the Navy to which I might have been drafted. However, as things developed I am convinced that Admiral Wake-Walker, who at that time was Rear Admiral Commanding Mine Layers, was right in his conception of things and it was largely due to his ideas that ultimately, after five to six months, the investigation section to work under the Director of Torpedoes and Mines, namely DTMI, was formed.

I well remember that at that time Captain Denis Boyd, who had been working as Number One to Admiral Wake-Walker, was about to leave for the Mediterranean in order to command the *Illustrious* which was newly commissioned. I begged him to take me with him but he said that I would be of more service to the Navy by continuing in the new investigation section. He spoke in the highest praise of Captain Maitland-Dougall who would be my new Chief, and prophesied that I should greatly enjoy working with him. I had come to respect Captain Denis Boyd very much indeed, not only as a naval officer but as a philosopher and man of culture. He was extremely widely read and had given great thought to such problems as comparative religions, and his reading, combined with his extensive service in the Royal Navy, made him an absorbing conversationalist and delightful company on those rare occasions when we were able to spend a quiet evening after dinner in the Senior United Services' Club.

After he left the Admiralty he went on to great achievements in the Mediterranean where he was to a large extent responsible for the famous air strike at Taranto, and where he fought the *Illustrious* through many battles, bringing her battered but nevertheless triumphant into Malta Harbour. Afterwards, of course, he went on to become Admiral Sir Denis Boyd, Commander-in-Chief in the Far East. To my regret our paths did not cross again during the rest of the war.

I have paid tribute in the course of the text to some of those officers who assisted from time to time. I remember with particular affection Captain Carslake who, although very fully occupied with his own job, would nevertheless always be willing to spare a moment to discuss the meaning of some particularly mysterious event with me. He was a man not only with wide experience as a Torpedo Officer, but had considerable outside scientific knowledge which he was always willing to place at our disposal. In addition, of course, there were the civilian scientists, working under the Director of Scientific Research, whose ideas were invaluable.

Through the privilege of being associated with Captain Maitland-Dougall I was able to meet many of the distinguished officers of the Service at one time or another. In particular, when Admiral Sir Henry Harwood returned to London from his great victory of the River Plate, he (at that time Commodore Harwood), came to see Captain Maitland-Dougall with whom he had been a shipmate of the same term in *Britannia* (the Naval Training School at Dartmouth), and I therefore had the pleasure of lunching with him within a day or two of his Victory March through London.

When final victory was achieved over Germany I volunteered to stay on in order to clear up the position in regard to enemy weapons in Kiel and Eckernförde in Northern Germany, and in fact I was retained in the Navy from October, 1945 until May, 1946. By the system of discharge which had been adopted I could, of course, have obtained my release in October, 1945, but I preferred, as far as possible, to complete the job I had been doing by this work in Germany. I was in fact offered by the Admiralty a further year's engagement in the rank of Commander as Torpedo Commander, Berlin, but I asked if I could be excused from taking up this appointment as I was by that time anxious to get back to my own civilian profession.

Looking back upon the years of my service with the Royal Navy, despite the inevitable strains and stresses of war service, the overall recollection is one of great pleasure and a feeling of gratitude for having had the privilege of serving. I suppose it is the common experience of all those who served during the war that it was an experience not to be missed: that it was an education in itself. One certainly learned to understand human nature and to realise what unexpected qualities of steadfastness and courage men possessed. There were also, of course, the invaluable friendships which I am happy to think have persisted into the years of peace.

Chapter 1

How it all Began

The minelayer *M.I.*, in from the sea, crept through the heavy darkness of blacked-out Portsmouth Harbour and made fast alongside the jetty of H.M.S. *Vernon*, the Royal Navy's Torpedo and Mining Establishment.

The time was 0130 on November 17th, 1939.

Hardly had the gangway been put aboard when I heard one of the berthing party call out: "Message for Lieutenant Lincoln."

I hurried down from the minelayer's bridge to find the rating who was calling my name.

"The Duty Commander wants to see you right away, sir."

I went ashore and cautiously groped my way along the unlit jetty through the clutter of minesweeping gear. I reached the officers' quarters and found the Duty Commander's cabin. I knocked on the door.

From the other side a sleepy voice said: "That you, Lincoln?"

"Yes, sir."

"Come in, but don't switch on the light – the blackout isn't drawn."

I entered, and the bed creaked as the Duty Commander hoisted himself up from his pillow.

He said: "You have to report to the Admiralty at once."

"What, now, sir?"

"What's the time?" he said.

"Getting on for two o'clock."

"First train in the morning, then."

"Do you know what it's about, sir?"

"You're some kind of lawyer, aren't you?"

"That's right, sir."

There was a pause, and then the voice in the darkness said: "All I know is that you are required to report to N.A.2S.L. forthwith. Good night."

I made my way back to the minelayer considerably puzzled by this turn of events. The immediate thought which had occurred to me was that the call to the Admiralty might mean I was going to get a seagoing command of my own, for, along with five others who had been trained at H.M.S. *Vernon* as mine specialists, I had been chosen in readiness to take over one of the new 500-ton loop minelayers when they became available. My present duties as acting First Lieutenant in minelayer *M.I* were merely a stop-gap in readiness for this duty. But, whatever the reason for the summons to Whitehall, I realised this was not the explanation. The new minelayers, which were being built in the West Country, were still not ready for commissioning. Besides, I should hardly be ordered to the Admiralty simply to be told that I was to assume command of one of them. A routine signal would be enough for that.

The identity of the department to which I had to report, N.A.2S.L., gave no hint as to what was behind the summons. In fact, I did not even know at that moment what the letters stood for. Even when I learned they were an abbreviation for Naval Assistant to the Second Sea Lord, I was still no wiser.

The most curious feature seemed to be the Duty Commander's question about my being a lawyer. He was not merely being conversational; it was not the sort of information which a Royal Naval officer, awakened in the middle of the night, would idly seek. The fact that he had raised the subject of my peacetime profession suggested that it had some bearing on whatever was in the offing.

The more I thought about it, the less I made of it. If the Admiralty wanted the services of a legally trained man, there must be plenty of elderly barristers on whom they could call, men whose age made them unsuited for active service at sea.

Already, I was beginning to feel a certain apprehension that the journey to London might interfere with my sea service. If there was any suggestion that this might be so, I would do everything possible to resist it. There had been nothing casual about my joining the Navy. It was something which had occupied my mind and energy for at least three years before the outbreak of the war, right from the time, in fact, when war seemed inevitable.

In 1936, I tried to join the Royal Naval Volunteer Reserve, but the top age limit then was twenty-five, and I was twenty-six. But as soon as I heard that the Royal Naval Volunteer (Supplementary) Reserve had been formed, I presented myself at the Admiralty. I was not a little proud of the fact that my Supplementary Reserve number was seventy-seven in a Reserve that numbered thousands. Next, I set about improving my seamanship. For a good many years I had been a keen yachtsman – a cruising man, that is; I have never much cared for racing – and so I had a fair practical knowledge of piloting and navigating small craft. First, I went to Captain O.M. Watts, of Albemarle Street, off Piccadilly, and got him to give me a course in coastal navigation. After that, I took a correspondence course on the multitude of subjects necessary to qualify for a Yacht Master's Certificate; apart from cargo handling, the range covered was very similar to that required in the qualifying examinations of Mercantile Marine ships' officers. In 1938, I reported to the Board of Trade and sat for my ticket, acquiring Yacht Master's Certificate No. 70. Shellbacks who learned their seamanship the hard way in Cape Horners may not approve such methods, but it was the best I could do in the time I could spare from building up my legal practice. And it was aimed with one goal in mind: to serve at sea in the Royal Navy when war came.

Whatever the outcome of the summons to the Admiralty was to be, I should only know when I got there. No amount of speculation could provide me with an answer. I turned into my bunk for what remained of the night to get a few hours' sleep before catching the early train up to London.

At Waterloo Station taxis were scarce and I was glad to share one with a Royal Naval lieutenant-commander who had also travelled up from Portsmouth on his way to the Admiralty. He introduced himself as Dick Ryan, lately torpedo officer of the cruiser *Berwick*, newly returned from the West Indies. I had seen and admired her lying alongside in Portsmouth Dockyard.

By a coincidence, Ryan also had to report to N.A.2S.L.

When we arrived at the office of this functionary, we were met by a commander who announced that he was to take us at once to Admiral Wake-Walker, the Rear-Admiral, Minelayers.

Ryan knew the Admiral. "He's quite a character," he said.

Never having met an admiral during my two months in the Navy, I felt at a slight disadvantage. However, as Ryan and I were ushered into Admiral Wake-Walker's room, I had no cause for alarm. The Admiral was a most impressive man, but he was in no way intimidating. He was six-feet-two tall, thin almost to the point of being skinny and gave the impression of abounding energy. His hair was fair, his eyes vividly blue and piercingly sharp.

He greeted Ryan, and then turned to me. "Hello, Lincoln. I hear you're a K.C. in civilian life. Is that right?"

"Not a K.C., sir, only a junior barrister."

"Same thing," said the Admiral briskly. "So long as you're some sort of lawyer and, of course, know something about mines."

He told us to sit down and straightway said: "Well, you chaps, the country is in dire peril."

So far, the circumstances of my call to London had been in the best traditions of romantic fiction: the urgent midnight summons, with its slightly mysterious undertones, the hurried journey to Whitehall and the meeting with an important personage who made a dramatic announcement before enlisting the aid of the person summoned. There had been a sense of unreality about it all. But this was not fiction. Nor was there anything unreal about what Admiral Wake-Walker was now saying. It was quite the most staggering statement I had ever heard.

He walked, long-legged, up and down the room, rapidly giving Ryan and me the facts.

At the start of the war, Hitler had threatened Britain with a secret weapon. Now it appeared that the threat was being fulfilled. Certainly, there was no doubt as to the deadly effectiveness of the weapon.

The Admiral said: "Most of our harbours and navigable rivers are being blocked by a mine of no known or conventional type. All efforts to sweep it have proved unavailing. The use of magnetic sweepers has been almost entirely unsuccessful. These have been tried out in areas known to be thickly mined, but only in one case, in the Bristol Channel, has a magnetic sweeper exploded a mine. Continued failure elsewhere seems to confirm this as a fluke. All efforts to recover the new mines with the aid of grapnels and nets have also failed."

To complete the picture, the Admiral turned towards the huge map of the British Isles which covered one wall of the room; most harbours and rivers were blocked; the whole of the East Coast waters were impassable; the Thames, Tees and Tyne were virtually closed to shipping owing to the fact that as vessels moved in these waters they were blown up; there were now something like 185 ships held up in the Downs (the southern approaches to the Thames) and another 70 immobilized in the London Docks.

He said: "Losses have now reached a total of six ships put out of action a day. This is a drain which cannot continue. In fact, if it cannot be checked England will be defeated in six weeks."

I was too completely taken aback by the Admiral's disclosures even to wonder why I, a very junior R.N.V.R. officer, should have been taken into his confidence in this fashion.

He went on: "It is absolutely vital that the nature of the weapon should be discovered and a successful antidote

5

invented. I have personally been appointed by the First Lord of the Admiralty to take charge of the investigation and produce an effective counter."

He outlined his arrangements. He had appointed Captain Denis Boyd, R.N., as his chief-of-staff. Captain Boyd had commanded the Torpedo School at H.M.S. *Vernon*, and so was one of the outstanding Naval authorities on underwater weapons.

Lieutenant-Commander George Norfolk was to be Staff Officer Operations. His task was to take charge of attempts to recover a specimen of the mine.

Dick Ryan, also a fully-qualified torpedo officer, was to handle the technical investigation.

At this stage, the Admiral had decided, because of the numerous conflicting reports on the mine, that he needed someone trained to weigh evidence, and had felt that a lawyer was best suited for the job. But his problem had been to find a lawyer who was also familiar with mines. When he spoke to Captain Boyd of the type of person he had in mind, Boyd recalled that there had been a barrister who had done the course at H.M.S. *Vernon*. This was how I had come to be chosen.

"Your role," said Wake-Walker, "will be to sift the evidence relating to the new mine in the mass of reports received from the masters and crews of ships that have been sunk or damaged and attempt to analyse its nature and qualities."

He added, addressing both Ryan and myself: "You will have to work night and day until we have this thing taped. Beds will be provided here at the Admiralty so that you can be on hand at all times. Now I suggest you have some lunch. I shall want you back in this office sharp at two."

Over a hurried luncheon, Ryan and I discussed our new jobs. The prospect did not at all please him.

"Just as I'm sweating on the top line to get my brass hat," he said, "this thing had to come along, and I'm taken from active service to do a blasted desk job!"

I sympathised with him. As a senior lieutenant-commander

he was in the zone for promotion to commander, but it was necessary that he should get in the maximum sea time before he got his "brass hat". He never did return to sea and realise his ambition. Just a year later, poor Dick Ryan met his death. By then the "blasted desk job" had long proved very different from anything that he and I had ever anticipated. Occupying a desk had very little to do with the job. Dick was killed attempting to render safe a particularly dangerous German mine. His gallantry was recognised by the posthumous award of the George Cross.

But all this was in the future. Our immediate concern was to get back to the Admiralty and find out how we were to go about our new duties.

Captain Boyd told us that we were both to attend a conference which had been called that afternoon. The assembly of gold braid was almost overwhelming. Even so the meeting was dominated by a stocky figure in dark civilian suit and spotted bow tie, Winston Churchill, First Lord of the Admiralty.

Churchill wanted to know what steps Wake-Walker had taken to solve the problem of the weapon which could bring Britain to disaster within six weeks.

The Admiral detailed what had so far been done, naming Commander Ryan as his new technical adviser and adding: "I have appointed a lawyer chap who is a mine expert to sift the evidence."

"Lawyer?" said Churchill, glaring over his spectacles. "Where is he?"

I rose from my seat at the back of the room to come under the scrutiny of the entire gathering. Churchill gave what sounded suspiciously like a grunt, and then returned to the business of the conference. I thankfully sat down again.

When the meeting ended, Ryan and I set to work. It was then that I realised my role was to be that of a detective.

Chapter 2

The First Magnetic Mine

Admiral Wake-Walker had warned me that the documentary evidence on the mysterious German mine was confusing, some of it even contradictory. This was not to be wondered at. The reports in the main were from masters and crews of ships which had fallen victim to the mine. Invariably, disaster had come on them without warning. It was a sudden, shattering experience.

Under the circumstances they could hardly be expected to make wholly objective observations of such technical details as concerned us. But, until we recovered one of the mines intact, all we had to go on were the experiences of those who had survived the ordeal of being blown up and the details of damage to ships which had not actually sunk. From this information we had to try to deduce the nature of the weapon and the way it worked.

There was no shortage of evidence. In a sheaf of reports handed to me by Captain Boyd there were dozens of individual accounts of sinkings. However much these varied in detail, two facts seemed to emerge pretty clearly. From the position of the ships involved, it seemed that the mine was rarely used in water more than twenty fathoms – 120 feet – deep. Secondly, the mines never came in actual contact with the ships.

At the start of the war, the conventional sea mine used by both ourselves and the Germans was a type which exploded on contact. It was spherical in shape and contained a charge of around 350 pounds of high explosive. On being laid by a minelayer it sank to the sea bed, staying there long enough for the minelayer to get clear, and then rose to a depth determined by the pre-set length of its anchor line. There it was anchored by a mooring cable attached to a sinker. The depth at which the mine floated was usually about ten feet below the surface, far enough down not to be readily detected but close enough to the surface to be struck by the hull of a passing ship. From the casing of the mine sprouted a number of horns, each containing a glass tube of acid. When a ship struck a mine, the impact smashed the glass tube inside one of the horns, the acid spilling on metallic plates caused an electric current which fired a detonator, and the mine exploded. This type was known as a "contact" mine.

There was no mistaking damage caused by the direct explosion of a contact mine. It blasted an enormous hole. More often than not the mine struck in the region of the bows and so the fore part of the ship was frequently shattered.

All the evidence we had on the mine we were seeking to master made it clear that it did not explode on contact. It might blow a ship clean out of the water, break her back and mangle the machinery, or it might buckle hull plates badly, nearly always causing the damage amidships and from below; but there never seemed to be any massive ripping away of plates. When there was a hole, it was usually quite small in size. This told us that the explosion occurred some distance beneath the ship.

Therefore, we reasoned, the explosion resulted from some influence exerted by the ship when she passed over the mine.

There were a number of possible influences.

Pressure was one. As a ship steamed on her course, there would be a downward pressure caused by her displacement. The pressure could affect the mine mechanism in such a way as to set it off. The fact that the mines were always laid in comparatively shallow water supported the pressure theory. In deep water, the pressure would not be so noticeable and so there would be no guarantee that the mine would explode.

I checked back through the reports. If explosions were touched off by pressure, the faster and larger a ship was the more vulnerable she would be because her passage through the water would create more downward pressure than that of a slower, smaller ship. But speed and size obviously had no bearing on losses: these included vessels of all kinds, large and small, fast and slow. The mine did not discriminate.

Pressure as a cause of explosion was crossed off the list.

Another suggestion was that mines were of the acoustic type. Water is a wonderful conductor of sound. Sound travels through water at 5,000 feet per second, compared with 1,100 feet per second through air at sea level. So a ship's engine and propeller noises transmitted down into the sea could set in operation the mechanism of an acoustic mine. As soon as the sound reached a certain volume, the mine would go off. Obviously, the volume of sound necessary to explode a mine would have to be set fairly low so that ships which operated reasonably silently should not escape. That being so, a particularly noisy ship would set off a mine while still some distance off. There were plenty of very noisy ships at sea around the coast of Britain; coasters with thumping, old-fashioned diesel engines that could be heard miles away; fast motor torpedo boats and destroyers which at speed produced considerable hull vibration. This meant that there should have been many explosions in the vicinity of ships as well as those which resulted in vessels being blown up.

But there was none. All reports on the mine we were attempting to tackle showed that it invariably blew up right under its victim.

It was not an acoustic mine.

In those early days there was one final cause which could be taken into practical account: magnetism. Was Hitler's "secret weapon" a magnetic mine?

Although the extent of our shipping losses was kept from the public, it was no secret that we were losing ships. Quite apart from the stories told by survivors to their families and friends when they came ashore, the fact that many thousands of dock workers and longshoremen were idle because of the virtual paralysis of shipping made the whole subject one for vital discussion in every waterfront bar in the country. The newspapers were not allowed to publish details of losses for security reasons, but they were able to speculate on the nature of Hitler's "secret weapon". Their guess was that it was a magnetic mine. The general impression was that the magnetism of the ship attracted the mine so that it rose through the water and exploded on coming into contact with the vessel's hull.

This we knew to be impossible. The amount of magnetic influence exerted by a ship's hull simply was not enough to achieve this. What it could do was to make active a magnetic needle in the mine which caused it to explode.

There was, in fact, quite a lot that we knew about magnetic mines. The Royal Navy used them in the North Sea in the First World War, and was now perfecting more advanced types at H.M.S. *Vernon*. Along with this development, a counter-measure had also been evolved to sweep magnetic mines. It consisted of a number of bar magnets strung onto a cable suspended between two vessels. It was still in a fairly experimental stage, and it was called the "Bo'sun's Nightmare". The reason it got the name was that as it dragged along the sea bed it often caught up in wrecks and fouled any snags it met and was, in consequence, a far from popular piece of gear.

Two trawlers using the "Bo'sun's Nightmare" in the Bristol Channel had exploded a mine. At least, they had exploded something. Was it a magnetic mine? Or was it merely a chance explosion of some other sort of mine by the sweep? The fact that it was the solitary success, despite the massive effort being made to clear shipping channels, put a very large question mark over the incident. The evidence was too isolated to make any conclusion possible.

Then, to complicate the whole situation still further, there was the strange story of the S.S. *Mandalay* of Glasgow. The *Mandalay*, a 5,000-ton merchantman, was lying at anchor inside Spurn Head on the Humber when she was blown up. Three members of the crew said that just before the blast of the explosion they heard a buzzing noise.

"It was like an electric sewing machine," they said.

At first we wondered whether the mine lay on the bottom and when the *Mandalay* swung on the tide the magnetic influence of the hull had caused some sort of guided missile to be released so that it rose under power to explode against the ship's bottom. But no other report received made any mention of sewing-machine noises, so we were inclined to dismiss these as just another sailor's yarn.

In doing so, we did less than justice to the three members of the crew of the sunken merchantman. Their observation had been perfectly accurate. It was not until long afterwards that we discovered the explanation. The sound they heard was that given off by a German electric torpedo when running shallow. What had happened was that a U-boat had slipped unobserved into the Humber, launched its torpedo and put to sea again without anyone realising just what was going on.

By and large, the evidence we had pointed to the fact that the mine we had to defeat was of the magnetic type. But we were still completely in the dark as to how to counter it. So far every attempt at sweeping had failed – discounting the doubtful business of the "Bo'sun's Nightmare" in the Bristol Channel.

The normal method of sweeping mines was to tow a serrated wire through the water. This cut the mooring cables and brought the mines bobbing up to the surface, where they could be exploded or sunk by gunfire. The advantage of moored magnetic mines was that they could be anchored much farther below the surface than the usual ten-foot depth of the horned contact mines, and so they were that much more difficult to sweep. But even when sweeps were carried out at greater depth, we still had no success. We were baffled.

It was then that I had an extraordinary piece of good luck, arising, ironically, from the misfortune of a merchant ship's crew.

The 10,500-ton tanker *James Maguire* was blown up. The force of the explosion hurled her bodily out of the water. But tankers are exceptionally strongly built. The *James Maguire* continued to float and was successfully towed into port.

Examination showed that running fore and aft along the bottom of the tanker was an enormous dent. This could not be measured with absolute accuracy because of the buckling of the plates, but it was estimated to be near enough 140 feet long.

The moment this fact came to light, I knew we were on to something important. One of the things I had learned at H.M.S. *Vernon* was that underwater explosions always behave in a predictable fashion owing to the fact that water cannot be compressed. The force of an explosion in water takes the form of a cone. The point of explosion is the apex of the cone, and the angle formed there is always a right angle.

So I drew a triangle with an apex of 90 degrees, and let its base represent 140 feet. By the most elementary geometry, a perpendicular dropped from the apex to the base equalled half the length of the base. From this simple calculation – Q.E.D. – the explosion occurred 70 feet under the *James Maguire*.

It was the first and only occasion in my life when I have found geometry of any practical value whatever.

The tanker's master was a careful seaman and had noted the precise position of his ship at the moment of the explosion. A quick check on the chart showed that, after making allowance for tidal variation, the depth of water at this spot was approximately 70 feet at the time.

Now we had conclusive proof that the mine was not moored at all: it lay on the sea bed. This explained why we had never been able to bring a mine to the surface by sweeping.

Recovery of a mine so that we could learn its secrets looked as if it was going to be a very difficult task indeed. But, quite suddenly, circumstances changed dramatically in our favour.

Luftwaffe mine-laying aircraft were busily operating off the East coast. This, incidentally, was a breach of International Law, which requires minefields to be properly defined and their whereabouts notified to neutral nations.

As a result of the indiscriminate minelaying, fifteen merchantmen were sunk in four days off the East Coast. The destroyer *Gipsy* was also sunk and the cruiser *Belfast* damaged. Two of the merchantmen were neutrals, the Japanese liner *Terukuni Maru* and the 8,000-ton Dutch liner *Simon Bolivar*. The Dutch ship was blown up south-east of Harwich with the loss of 138 lives.

A desperate expedient was decided upon. Admiral Wake-Walker put his plan to Nore Command and on November 22nd the Commander-in-Chief, Nore, sent this signal to the captain of the destroyer *Wivern*:

> When ordered H.M.S. *Wivern* is to carry out four runs at full speed down the line from wreck of *Simon Bolivar* in position 51 degrees 49.6 minutes North, 01 degrees 41 minutes East and wreck of British ship *Blackhill* in position 51 degrees 47.6 minutes North, 01 degrees 39 minutes East. It is expected that ship's passage will detonate mines and that owing to delayed action pistol mines will detonate astern of ship. Trawlers *Wellard* and *Lady Elsa* now on patrol D are to be used to embark all officers and men who can be spared and to stand by. If practicable no one is to be below deck or in engine room or boiler room. Number of mines detonated is to be reported by wireless.

I do not know what the reaction of the *Wivern's* captain was to this instruction. To get orders that you are deliberately to risk being blown out of the water by chasing up and down what is believed to be a thickly-sewn minefield cannot be very agreeable. The very fact that the order was given, involving the lives of highly-trained seamen and the possible loss of a much-needed destroyer, showed how critical the situation was. However drastic, a method of clearing the sea bed of mines simply had to be found.

With luck, *Wivern's* speed would carry her clear before a mine went off. But she would need all her speed and all her luck. It was going to be a perilous task.

Wivern carried out the instructions, with the two trawlers standing by ready to pick up survivors if the worst happened.

Nothing in fact happened. The four runs were made, but no mines were detonated.

That night, however, the Luftwaffe returned. Coast watchers saw a Heinkel 115 fly in close to the Essex shore of the Thames Estuary at Shoeburyness, beyond Southend-on-Sea. A few moments later a parachute dropped towards the mud flats. The first reaction of the men on coast watch was that they had seen a parachutist land. They tried to reach the spot where the airman, as they believed, had come down, but already the tide was flooding over the flats and they could not get through the rising water.

The news of the parachute descent was immediately linked with reports of Luftwaffe activity the night before. Aircraft had flown in over the Thames and Stour estuaries and the Humber dropping mines by parachute. It was quite clear that the Shoeburyness "parachutist" was in fact a magnetic mine. And it had fallen in a position where it could be reached.

The German pilot had obviously never spent a holiday at Southend, or he would have known that he should keep well away from that shore. The tide in those parts ebbs so far that the water vanishes from sight of land. As soon as the tide receded, the magnetic mine would be exposed.

Lieutenant-Commander J.G.D. Ouvry, of H.M.S. *Vernon*, who had been standing by in London, was summoned to the Admiralty shortly after midnight. Mr. Churchill himself was in at the briefing.

Ouvry's orders were quite simple: "The mine must be recovered at all costs."

He was an expert, a professional, and he knew what the implications of the order could be to himself. He set off immediately for Shoeburyness by car, accompanied by Lieutenant-Commander R.C. Lewis, another *Vernon* officer who had been standing by in London.

At Shoeburyness, as the tide went down, they examined the mine by torchlight. It was cylindrical in shape and about six-feet-six long. It was photographed by flashlight and its external characteristics were noted in detail. When daybreak came, it was discovered that there was a second mine lying three hundred yards from the first.

Both Ouvry and Lewis were fully aware of what was at stake: the whole course of the war might turn on their success or failure. From an individual point of view, failure could only have one possible outcome: final and utter obliteration.

Ouvry, it was decided, should first tackle the mine. He had worked out exactly every move he would make, and he detailed these in the strict order in which he proposed to make them so that, from farther up the beach, Lewis could watch him and know at each stage precisely what he was doing. In this way, if Ouvry made a fatal mistake, Lewis would know what he had done wrongly and so could avoid that particular error when he came to tackle the second mine. The discovery of the second mine had given them a double chance of success. If one failed, the other might succeed.

Ouvry and Chief Petty Officer Baldwin, who had brought a mine recovery team up from H.M.S. *Vernon*, checked that they had taken all metal articles from their clothing and set off together down the beach and across the flats. They were armed with non-magnetic tools.

They successfully removed a detonator from the mine. But they now had to get to its underside which had sunk into the muddy sand, so Lewis and A.B. Vearncombe joined them to turn over the deadly contraption.

Up on the safety of the foreshore, the remainder of the recovery party stared out across the sullen flats to the spot where the four men crouched at their task. The mine might be fitted with a booby trap. At any stage in the operation their tampering with the mechanism could spring the trap. The watchers waited, aware of nothing but the utter isolation of the four men calmly involved in what might be their last act.

But, eventually, the job was done. A second detonator had been discovered and removed. The mine was safe.

It had taken three interminable hours.

The mine was loaded on to a lorry and driven to H.M.S. *Vernon* where experts were waiting to conduct the post mortem examination. In twelve hours their full, detailed report reached the Admiralty.

The mine was perfectly safe while in the aircraft that carried it, but when it was dropped a bomb fuse was armed, a pilot chute was opened and this in turn opened the main parachute. On impact, a small weight was made to slide in the bomb fuse and start a fuse clock working. This ran for twenty seconds. When it stopped, the mine was supposed to blow up – unless it was in sixteen or more feet of water. Then hydrostatic pressure operated a spring-loaded plunger and stopped the clockwork. After seventeen minutes in deep water, the arming clock blew a fuse which released the magnetic needle and then the mine was fully armed, its 660-pound explosive charge ready to blow up any ship passing immediately above it. But if the mine were to be hauled up to a depth of less than sixteen feet the spring-loaded plunger stopping the fuse clock automatically withdrew, the clockwork mechanism started again and the mine exploded.

In short, it was designed to defy any attempt at recovery.

We had been amazingly fortunate to recover two of the mines in which, by some curious chance, the ingenious, complicated and seemingly foolproof mechanism had failed to destroy them before they could be made safe. For their action in making safe the first mine, Ouvry and Lewis were awarded the D.S.O., and Baldwin and Vearncombe were awarded the D.S.M.

Now we knew everything there was to know about the magnetic mine – everything, that is, except how to overcome it.

Admiral Wake-Walker called an immediate conference of the most outstanding civilian and Naval scientists in this particular sphere. They included Dr. Wright, the Director of Scientific Research, and his advisers, Dr. A.B. Wood, the Principal Scientific Officer in the Mine Design Department, Lieutenant-Commander (later Professor Sir Charles) Goodeve, R.N.V.R., who was then serving in H.M.S. *Vernon*, and Professor Bernard Haigh, Professor of Applied Mechanics at the Royal Naval College, Greenwich.

The Admiral told the conference there were two problems to be solved: first, how to protect our merchant ships; secondly, how to design an adequate sweep. Of the two, the first was the more urgent, because it was absolutely vital that shipping should be given immunity.

"Is it possible," he asked, "to demagnetize a ship?"

The question led to a long and anxious discussion. Finally the scientists gave their considered opinion. They would need a year of experiment, and even then they could not guarantee to produce the answer.

Scientifically speaking, they were, of course, right; they were considering the complete demagnetizing of a ship, which is almost impossible to achieve. But obviously something had to be produced in far short of a year, even if it was less than scientifically perfect.

As the meeting broke up, Wake-Walker said to Captain Boyd: "What the scientists can't do, perhaps a Naval officer can."

He turned to me: "Lincoln, get on the phone to *Vernon* and tell them to wind an energized coil round a ship and try that out."

I put through the call and spoke to Dick Ryan, who had gone to work in H.M.S. *Vernon* for a time. As I passed on the Admiral's message, Ryan chuckled.

He said: "That idea has already occurred to us. We're experimenting with it now."

Chapter 3

Early Detective Work

As the technical people worked night and day on counter-measures, we at the Admiralty were kept fully occupied on the investigation side. During December, I was sent up to the north-east coast to investigate the disaster which engulfed a coastal convoy bound from Methil to the Thames.

The convoy had been held up by thick fog close to St. Mary's Island, near Whitley Bay. As soon as the fog cleared, the ships got under way. In two days, fourteen of them were sunk by unexplained explosions.

In his report on the convoy sinkings, the Flag Officer in charge of the Tyne Area gave his opinion that the ships had been torpedoed, but magnetic mines could also have been the cause.

One of the shattered ships, the 9,000-ton tanker *Inverlane*, had been beached at Roker, near Sunderland. I went there to examine her. The broken hull lay forlornly on the deserted sands of the little peacetime resort. From the damage I knew that the *Inverlane* had been struck by a contact weapon, either mine or torpedo, but certainly not a magnetic mine.

It seemed to me from the very number of sinkings and the fact that they had all occurred in the same area that it was unlikely that a U-boat had been responsible. It would be highly improbable that a submarine commander would hang around and risk detection after making a successful kill. A much more likely explanation, I thought, was that the convoy had steamed into a newly laid minefield. The fog which held up the convoy could have supplied the opportunity for the enemy to slip in, lay the mines and put out to sea again before anyone suspected they had been there.

As there was nothing more to learn at Roker, I went on to try to seek more evidence on Tyneside.

At the time of the convoy disaster, the destroyers *Kelly* and *Mohawk* were lying in the Tyne where they were undergoing repairs. The *Kelly* was commanded by Lord Louis Mountbatten, who was also Captain (D) of the Fifth Destroyer Flotilla belonging to the Home Fleet. On the chance that a U-boat might have been responsible for the massacre of the convoy, Mountbatten immediately put to sea with the two destroyers. They headed for the scene at full speed, determined if possible to make a kill. Soon they sighted the blazing tanker *Athel Templar*, one of the victims. As the *Kelly* slowed down to make an asdic sweep, a shattering explosion turned the destroyer's stern into a concertina of torn and twisted metal. The *Kelly* began to make water and go down by the stern. Commander Eaton in the *Mohawk* put lines aboard and towed the crippled *Kelly* back to the Tyne.

She was now in dry dock at Messrs. Hawthorn Leslie's yard at Hebburn, where she had been built. It was there that I went to see what I could learn from Lord Louis Mountbatten.

If the Captain of a Home Fleet destroyer flotilla thought it rather odd that the "Admiralty expert" sent up to provide the answer to the mystery sinkings should turn out to be rather a junior R.N.V.R. lieutenant, he showed no sign of it. He received me kindly and told me all he could about the explosion which had damaged his ship.

Just before it occurred, he and the other officers on the bridge heard something bump the ship's side immediately beneath them. A moment later another bump sounded farther aft. The third bump was followed by the explosion.

"The knocks against the hull and the subsequent explosion could not have been caused by a magnetic mine," I said. "The damage was obviously the result of the blast of a contact weapon."

"How do you know it wasn't a torpedo?" asked Mountbatten.

"Well, I could not say that it wasn't, sir. May I have a closer look at the damage?"

He took me down into the dry dock and we walked all round the crippled destroyer examining her hull carefully. On the starboard side beneath the bridge a deep scratch scored the steel plating. Farther aft was a similar scar. Then we came to the shattered stern compartment. The propellers, though badly distorted, were more or less intact. I noticed that a piece had been chipped out of one blade. The damage could have been caused by the rotating propeller striking the mooring cable of a mine. German mines were also fitted with a device which could be set to ensure that an explosion occurred when tension came off the mooring cable, and this would account for the blast immediately after the third bump.

With a torch I made a minute examination of the buckled remains of *Kelly*'s once graceful stern. Presently I found the final piece of evidence I needed. Part of the horn of a contact mine was embedded in the ship's plating, driven there by the force of the explosion.

Now there was no doubt as to what had caused such destruction to the convoy and put *Kelly* out of action.

At once minesweepers were sent to the scene of the convoy sinkings. They swept up no fewer than 140 mines. One mine was recovered intact. It was made safe by Lieutenant R.S. Armitage, R.N.V.R., an expert from H.M.S. *Vernon*, who was later to receive both the George Medal and the George Cross for his exceptional courage in dealing with mines.

The mine was a type new to us. It contained about 600 pounds of explosive, nearly twice as much as in the earlier German contact mines we had recovered.

It was not till after the war that we obtained confirmation of how the minefield happened to be there. Enemy records showed that, as I had suspected, destroyers had crept in under cover of the fog and laid the mines.

21

My next investigation took me down to Falmouth where the tanker *Caroni River* had been sunk in mysterious circumstances.

In the report we had from the Minesweeping Captain on the staff of the Naval Commander-in-Chief at Plymouth, there were a number of puzzling features, the most striking of which was that the tanker had been blown up in a channel to the south-west of Falmouth Bay which had been regularly swept and was supposed to be clear of mines.

The weather was far from agreeable for a trip to the West Country: it was bitterly cold, the countryside lay deep in snow, and roads were icebound. But it had been even less agreeable for the men of the *Caroni River*.

When my train reached Plymouth, I was met by a car which had been sent from Naval Headquarters at Mount Wise. There I met Captain G.L. Hodson, R.N., the Minesweeping Captain. He was in his sixties and had retired from the Navy long before the war, but had been recalled on the outbreak of hostilities. During his active service days he had been a specialist in torpedoes and mining and was a very able and courageous officer.

Together we discussed the case of the *Caroni River*, and then drove over to Falmouth where the survivors from the tanker had been assembled at the naval base. I questioned them all. When I completed my interrogation, I was convinced that their ship had been sunk by a magnetic mine.

If this was so, we were faced with a new problem. So far, all magnetic mines appeared to have been dropped by enemy aircraft. But there had been no reports of any aircraft in the vicinity of Falmouth, nor had there been any trace of the big parachutes by which they were dropped into the sea. The most likely alternative explanation was that the mine had been laid by a U-boat.

Falmouth Bay is quite shallow, and so the type of U-boat used would be fairly small to make detection less likely. We knew that the Germans had a number of submarines of about 250 to 300 tons displacement intended for operating in coastal waters. They were handy little craft and it was perfectly possible for them to lay mines from their torpedo tubes. They had three tubes: two at the bow and one aft. It was the thought of these tubes which made me realise, suddenly, that we had a full-scale job on our hands.

Obviously, if the U-boat had entered Falmouth Bay to lay magnetic mines it had not merely deposited the one which had sunk the *Caroni River*. It had laid as many as it could carry. Now the standard length of a submarine's torpedo tube is 24 feet. We knew from the recovery by Ouvry and Lewis of the airborne magnetic mine dropped at Shoeburyness that the weapon was between six and seven feet long. Assuming that the submarine laid mines which were the same length, this meant that each torpedo tube could carry three magnetic mines, and the U-boat's total cargo could be nine mines.

Therefore, eight mines might still be lying out in the south-west channel of the bay, making it a death trap.

The basis of my assumption was, of course, pure guesswork, but it turned out to be of the inspired variety. Three months later when the German trawler *Polaris* was captured off Norway her cargo included five magnetic mines fitted for laying by submarine. A check showed that they would be carried three to a torpedo tube.

Meanwhile, I had no proof, only suspicion. But, if the situation was as I suspected, it had to be resolved swiftly, or more good men and precious ships would go to the bottom. The way to approach the problem, I decided, was to try to put myself in the position of the German U-boat commander, to think as he would have to think and see what resulted.

Obviously, his orders would be to block the entrance to Falmouth, and so the mines must be laid in a barrier across the swept channel in the harbour approaches.

How would he go about it? There were two standard methods he could have used to lay the mines: dogleg or diagonal. The quicker and safer method was a diagonal lay. As he was operating in hostile waters, he would go for speed and safety. He would use the diagonal lay.

For both minelaying methods, a prominent point ashore or some other mark would be needed for the U-boat commander to fix his position. It would have to be a mark visible at night, for he would have approached during darkness to avoid the risk of being seen. To view the situation as it had appeared through his eyes, I decided a short night cruise in one of the minesweeping trawlers based on Falmouth was necessary.

That night, Captain Hodson and I boarded a trawler and put to sea.

We headed out into the channel in clear moonlight. After we had cleared the coast the trawler swung round and steamed slowly back towards the land.

Although much of what we were going on was pure speculation, we had one firm fact: the wreck of the *Caroni River* unquestionably marked the spot where a magnetic mine had been laid. The diagonal lay must pass through the wreck, which was marked by a cross on our chart. If we worked from the cross we could try to guess the position of the rest of the mines.

In the moonlight we sighted St. Anthony's Head standing out unmistakably. It was on this, I felt sure, that the U-boat commander had fixed his position, on this and the flashing light of the Manacles Buoy. The trawler skipper lined up St. Anthony's Head with the Manacles Buoy light until we had obtained a diagonal line running through the position in which the tanker had been sunk.

The line was carefully marked off on the chart. Here, I believed, was the direct pointer to the remainder of the U-boat's cargo of magnetic death.

"In my view, sir," I suggested to Hodson, "we should start sweeping along that line first thing in the morning."

He agreed.

It was not going to be an easy task. The scientists at H.M.S. *Vernon* were still deep in the problem of devising a really effective magnetic sweep. All that was generally available at the moment was a device called the "skid". This was usually a barge which carried an energized coil of wire. It was towed by a trawler.

The main snag with this method was that, since the trawler was in no way protected, she might set off the mine before the "skid" reached the spot. Apart from that, each time a mine was successfully exploded it usually meant the destruction of the "skid". This was nothing compared with the loss of merchantmen, but even so the average cost of a barge and coil was around £3,000. So it was an expensive method of sweeping and one that wasted a great deal of time, for the water covered by each barge was only the width of the beam of the barge.

Hodson had a number of "skids" available in Falmouth, and with these he prepared to set to work next day. I was looking forward keenly to see how justified my theories would turn out to be. However, I was unable to do so at first hand. Each stage of the investigation had to be telephoned to Admiral Wake-Walker, and when I asked to stay on to see the result of the sweep he said it would not be possible. He wanted me back at the Admiralty. It was a bitter disappointment, but there was nothing to do but return to London.

A few days later we had Captain Hodson's full report.

He had started off from a point near St. Anthony's Head with the first "skid" in tow and steamed out towards the Manacles Buoy on the line running through the *Caroni River*'s position, closely following the course we marked on the chart during our night reconnaissance. Suddenly, abruptly, the barge at the end of the tow line rose skywards, disintegrating from the thunderous impact of an exploding magnetic mine. In all, eight mines were safely detonated along the line I had charted.

So that no other U-boat commander might have such a convenient "fix" for laying mines again, the light on the Manacles Buoy was extinguished.

The "skids" which Hodson used to clear Falmouth harbour of magnetic mines were purely a stop-gap method. Other more effective and less hazardous systems were being developed.

While the Navy had been busy perfecting its own magnetic mine before the war, parallel work had gone on to produce a counter-measure. There were high hopes for success from a mine-destructor ship which had been designed early in 1939, H.M.S. *Borde*. She had a 400-ton electro-magnet mounted in her bows which could create a magnetic field capable of exploding a mine some distance ahead. Now she was brought into service and several other vessels were similarly equipped. But their success was limited. The British magnetic mine worked on a horizontal field, and the *Borde* was perfectly capable of dealing with that. But the German mine had a vertical field and was aimed to blow up any ship passing immediately above it. The result was that mines did not always blow up a safe distance ahead of the *Borde*-type ships. Some of them were damaged and their crews suffered alarming experiences. Again, like the "skid", it was too dangerous and costly a counter-measure.

What really proved to be the answer was supplied by Lieutenant-Commander Goodeve and Professor Haigh from Greenwich. They evolved a device consisting of a length of buoyant insulated cable towed astern of a minesweeper. At regular intervals a powerful electric current pulsed through the cable. When two sweepers steamed abreast a certain distance apart, each towing one of these cables, they could create a magnetic field between them capable of exploding any magnetic mines lying in their path. At first the device was known as the Haigh-Goodeve Sweep, but later it became simply the Double-ell (*LL*).

Admiral Wake-Walker's orders for tests by H.M.S. *Vernon* with a wire coil wound round a ship and energized by an electric current had produced completely satisfactory results. Experiments made with a trawler, a sloop, and a destroyer showed that by this method a ship's magnetic field could be reduced sufficiently to give some immunity against magnetic mines.

The coil became known as a "degaussing girdle". It was a misnomer to talk about degaussing, for the gauss – named after the nineteenth-century German scientist Carl Gauss – is merely a unit of measurement, but it enabled the irrepressible Dick Ryan to remark during the *Vernon* experiments: "I think the whole thing is a wild gauss chase!"

The Germans had possessed the magnetic mine for eight years, and during that time they had failed to evolve a counter-measure to it. They were convinced, not unreasonably, that we also should fail to find the answer before disastrous shipping losses forced us to defeat. Fortunately, in a few short weeks, we had discovered how to master Hitler's "secret weapon".

During the early days, the Navy was lamentably short of the necessary minesweeping gear. More powerful electrical equipment was needed for the minesweeping trawlers to enable them to generate the strong current pulses necessary to operate effectively the Double-ell sweep. Nor could enough of the special kind of buoyant cable for the sweep be produced to meet the demand. The reason for this was that the manufacturers were being pressed to produce something like 1,500 miles of cable a week to be used in "degaussing girdles" for our merchant ships.

But now it had become an industrial problem, not a matter of investigation.

By January, 1940, we had recovered a magnetic mine and an antidote was in hand. The original task for which I had been brought to the Admiralty was completed. I wanted to feel a ship's deck under my feet again, to return to the war at sea.

I went to ask Admiral Wake-Walker if this could now be arranged.

He shook his head. "I'm sorry, Lincoln. But the magnetic mine is not the only new weapon the Germans are going to use. We shall need you and a special investigation section to deal with the others as they come along."

And so I remained a "secret weapon" detective.

Chapter 4

DTM Investigation Section is Formed

When a new section was set up at the Admiralty to investigate German underwater weapons – it was known as the Directorate of Torpedoes and Mining (Investigations), or DTMI for short – I hoped to be put in charge. Having been in at the start of this somewhat specialised work, I felt I had earned the post. At the same time it was quite clear that if we were to carry weight in our dealings with other departments, an officer of greater seniority and rank should have command. The officer chosen was Captain Arnold Maitland-Dougall, R.N., who was brought back from retirement specially for the job.

Maitland-Dougall was over six feet tall and spare of build. He had somewhat cold blue-grey eyes and his manner was brusque. But any initial impression that he was either cold or off-hand soon vanished. He was in fact a very warmhearted person with a wonderful facility for handling men. In part this was due to his mature wisdom, still more to his essential humanity.

On one occasion, when a member of our section was killed while trying to make a mine safe, it so happened that Maitland-Dougall had managed to get a couple of seats at the theatre. He took the tickets from his pocket and laid them on his desk.

"Well, that's off, anyway," he said.

I knew how much he had been looking forward to his evening at the theatre and tried to persuade him to go; he was working under constant strain and needed the relaxation.

"After all," I said, "in war you have to accept that people get killed. But things must go on."

"No, I don't feel like the theatre, not now."

He picked up the tickets. "Here, you have them. You go."

I went, and next day he said: "Well, how did you enjoy the show?"

"Not very much. I kept thinking about poor————"

The incident of the theatre tickets made me realise how deep and genuine a concern Maitland-Dougall had for those who served under him. It was this that enabled him to deal with them so successfully.

He had one remarkable peculiarity. When you put a problem to him, he would never give an immediate answer but in silence would churn the facts over in his mind, considering them from every aspect. Sometimes the silence lasted so long that you had the impression he had not heard the question. But when the answer came it was decisively to the point and one, you felt, that was invariably right.

The basis of his judgment was a tremendous degree of skill acquired from very thorough technical training and long experience. He was a torpedo specialist and had been a torpedo-man in the Battle of Jutland. In the 'twenties he had been Mines Commander in H.M.S. *Vernon*.

I was extremely pleased to find myself second-in-command to such a man. I formed a deep respect and lasting affection for him.

The scope of our work was wide. Not only were we expected to keep track of any modifications and improvements in existing enemy mines and torpedoes, but we had to try to gather information on any new underwater weapons the Germans were developing – if possible, before they went into use. Later, we were given the job of finding out all we could about their mine-sweeping methods so that our designers could devise mines the Germans would be unable to sweep. All the time it was a contest to keep at least one jump ahead of the enemy.

As in any other detection work, we set about building up as complete a network of contacts as possible. Apart from the

Navy's own technical experts on mines and torpedoes, there were plenty of sources in the three Services which would be likely to come across the sort of information which might prove useful to us: the various intelligence branches, bomb disposal units, the R.A.F. specialists in enemy air weapons and the R.A.F. and Army interrogators of enemy prisoners at Cockfosters, Middlesex. Any chance scrap of information might give us a lead to a new development, or it might complete a link in a chain of evidence we had been gathering.

One example of the sort of help we were able to get from the R.A.F., for instance, arose over the shortage of Double-ell sweeping equipment. In the early days only two mine-sweeping flotillas were fitted with this gear, and this greatly increased the difficulty of dealing with magnetic mines.

The Germans were now laying the mines by Ju-52 aircraft. One night they might visit the Humber or the Thames Estuary, and then suddenly they would switch their attention to the West Country, laying mines at Portland, Milford Haven or in the Bristol Channel. With such limited sweeping equipment, it would clearly be an enormous advantage to discover when the Luftwaffe was going to operate in the North Sea and when operations were going to be carried out down Channel.

At the Air Ministry, I learned, there was an intelligence section known as A.I.3.(B), one of the functions of which was to seek to discover the whereabouts of every Luftwaffe squadron and the nature of its duties. The officer in charge of the section I was told was Wing-Commander Asher Lee, a name which sounded familiar to me. My first cousin, whom I had not seen for many years, was also named Asher Lee. When I went along to see the Wing-Commander, he proved to be my cousin.

He explained that the R.A.F. knew which particular German squadrons were employed on magnetic minelaying. When they were going to visit our East Coast, they operated from Schiphol in Holland. If the west coast was to be attacked, the aircraft were transferred to an airfield in Normandy.

From then on, as soon as he got wind of a minelaying squadron movement, he would ring me up to pass on the information. Immediately, we would warn the Minesweeping Section where they might expect the next minelaying operation, and they would arrange from the slender resources at hand that adequately equipped minesweeping forces were deployed in the threatened areas in advance.

Later, when the minesweeping forces which operated from every port of consequence were fully equipped to deal with every kind of enemy mine, these early warnings were no longer of such importance.

We had another piece of good fortune in the early days when a notebook taken from a captured German rating fell into our hands. In it was a little table he had compiled, down one side of which ran a series of letters – *EMA, EMB, EMC, EMD, LMA, LMB, LMC, LMD*, and so on. Along the top of the table were further letter symbols. One of these was *KG*, which we at once guessed meant kilogrammes. There were others, such as *LAD*, which stood for explosive charge. Beneath these letters representing charges in kilogrammes were a series of numbers, each opposite one of the sets of letters running down the side of the table. As the captured rating came from a minelayer, it seemed reasonable to assume that the table dealt with mines. We knew the size of the explosive charges in those German mines we had already recovered. By comparing these with the figures given in the notebook we were able to decide that *EMA*, for instance, was one of the standard horned moored mines. *EMA*, therefore, was the code name for *Einheits Minen A*. The *LM* series were the *Luft Minen*, the aircraft mines; *TM* stood for *Torpedorohr Minen*, literally, torpedo-tube mines, in other words submarine-laid mines. A number of the references were to mines which up till then we did not even know existed.

But the work of DTMI was not solely a backroom battle of wits, a matter of theorising: there was the strictly practical business of physically investigating German weapons when these fell into our hands. Generally this happened when the weapons failed to operate as had been intended. Foreseeing this possibility, the enemy attempted the most ingenious precautions to make our job as difficult – and risky – as possible. And so we had always to be prepared for the unexpected.

The only preparation was to learn all we could about minelaying, minesweeping, torpedoes and explosives. It was on this knowledge that our usefulness to the Navy depended and, on final reckoning, our individual prospects of survival. Gradually, we built up a team, mainly of Reserve officers, so that we had three specialists on mines and two on torpedoes. I spent some time in H.M.S. *Vernon* learning the latest techniques in making underwater weapons safe, and I trained some of our team in investigation methods.

As a result, one become known as an "Admiralty expert". Faith in the "Admiralty expert" was profound, and the responsibility that went with the title was sometimes quite awesome, as I discovered in March, 1940, when I was sent to Scapa Flow.

The Luftwaffe had been in action around the Orkneys and were thought to have dropped parachute mines in the Hoy entrance to the anchorage – the main, indeed the only entrance for the battlefleet. The minesweeping commander at Scapa had no experience of magnetic mines, nor had he Double-ell sweeps to deal with them, only "skids". So I was sent there to do the best I could.

Since the previous October when Kapitänleutnant Gunther Prien took the submarine *U-47* through the narrow entrance of Kirk Sound and torpedoed the battleship *Royal Oak* anchored in Scapa Flow, the Home Fleet had anchored elsewhere while the defences were strengthened. Now this had been done, the Fleet was steaming round from the Clyde. The First Lord of the Admiralty had embarked in H.M.S. *Rodney*, flagship of the Commander-in-Chief, Admiral Sir Charles Forbes, and was coming up to see Scapa Flow for himself.

With the arrival of Mr. Churchill and the Home Fleet imminent, I set to work. The trouble was that all we had for the task were "skids" similar to those used by Captain Hodson when he exploded the eight magnetic mines at Falmouth. But this time, we had no idea where the mines, if any, had been laid. The only way to be sure was to scour every inch of Hoy Sound. The "skid" was by no means the most reassuring method there was for such a task. It could only be certain of setting off mines immediately beneath it, and so the path it swept on any one run was limited to the beam of the barge carrying the energized coil – a matter of twenty feet. To make sure that there was an overlap of the swept paths was well nigh impossible. Tide, currents and wind all combined to make it more difficult. There was no guarantee that a narrow gap had not been left, and in that un-swept gap there might well be a magnetic mine.

For hour after barren hour we steamed up and down and around the forbidding, chilly Sound, dragging the "skid" behind us. But we did not detect a single mine.

Word came that the Home Fleet was rapidly approaching and that the Commander-in-Chief would expect to pass safely into Scapa Flow with his ships and distinguished guest.

In the back of my mind was the growing fear that the Germans had thought up some new way to foil us. They might now have fitted their mines with a delaying mechanism, which could be harmlessly actuated a number of times by the passage of a magnetic sweep and then, when all suspicion was gone, finally explode the mine under some luckless vessel. (Such devices – we called them "Clickers" – were later introduced by the enemy.) With such doubts troubling me, I decided we must have more time before we dared take the responsibility of declaring Hoy Sound clear of danger.

At our request, the Flag Officer in charge of the base sent a warning signal to the Commander-in-Chief. Admiral Forbes, who was now within sight of the Orkneys, decided that the Fleet should stand off for twenty-four hours while we continued our mine hunt. The ships altered course to the eastward.

The change, however, did not suit Mr. Churchill. He was anxious to get ashore. He did not want to be absent too long from the Admiralty in London.

Admiral Forbes offered to send him into harbour on board one of the destroyers. He accepted. But as he was about to transfer from the flagship an air raid alarm sounded. Ships' companies raced to action stations. The *Rodney* had meanwhile slowed down ready for the First Lord to transfer to a destroyer. This made her particularly vulnerable to any U-boat which might be lying in wait for just such an opportunity to launch a torpedo. In order not to expose the battleship to the risk any longer than necessary, Mr. Churchill hurriedly descended into a boat and was rowed across to the nearby destroyer. The vessel sped off to Scapa, entering the anchorage through what was known as the "tradesman's entrance", the small and narrow channel of Switha Sound to the south of Hoy Island which the destroyers customarily used.

We desperately went on with our sweeping of the Sound with the "skid". But by next day we still had failed to detonate a single mine.

"I suspect none has ever been dropped," I said to the minesweeping commander.

"You're the Admiralty representative, Lincoln," he said. "On your head be it if all is not well."

The responsibility for giving the all-clear was passed back to me. Convinced now that the vital channel must be clear, I boldly gave the word. The signal went to the waiting Commander-in- Chief.

The boom guarding the anchorage was opened in readiness. The Fleet turned about. There were something like seventy warships, including battleships, aircraft-carriers, cruisers and destroyers. In line ahead they steamed in towards the anchorage, a magnificent and majestic procession.

But to me the more memorable impression was not the majesty of the Home Fleet, but the sheer, utter relief when all the ships had steamed safely through the waters of the Sound. This must have been the only occasion during the entire war when a British battlefleet had been compelled to wait upon the decision of a junior R.N.V.R. officer before being permitted to enter harbour!

German Intelligence had clearly been well aware of the Fleet's movements, for that evening a full-scale Luftwaffe attack was delivered on Scapa Flow. As the bombers roared over, every ship in the anchorage erupted in a storm of ack-ack fire. Down came the bombs. The cruiser *Norfolk* was hit and heeled over, spurting columns of black smoke.

I was on board the depot ship *Greenwich*, but the trawler we had used for minesweeping operations was lying alongside. I scrambled on board the trawler and we cast off ready to go to the assistance of the *Norfolk*, but even as we did so the cruiser signalled to say that an oil fire, started by a bomb, was now under control and no help was needed. Shortly after, I was summoned aboard the *Rodney*, where the Commander-in-Chief had received reports that parachute mines had been dropped in the anchorage. He wanted the reports investigated.

In the trawler I made the rounds of the anchored ships, questioning those who had reported seeing parachute mines descending. The parachutes, they all said, were white or brown in colour. However, I knew that the Germans invariably used green parachutes for their magnetic mines.

Soon I was able to establish that the "parachutes" spotted had in fact been no more than slowly dispersing smoke puffs from ack-ack shell bursts! This was not as extraordinary as it might appear. The shells were bursting up under the aircraft, and as the planes continued on their course the trailing white smoke puffs could well be mistaken for parachutes. Even so, Admiral Forbes was taking no chances. He wanted a sweep of the waters around his flagship next day.

All the following day we swept round the battleship. There was a high wind blowing, and I noticed a rating standing right forward on the flagship's long fo'c'sle idly watching our efforts. Suddenly, a gust of wind caught his cap and blew it into the water. He gazed down helplessly at the floating cap, and abruptly his look of dismay turned to one of complete disbelief. For, in a sudden swirl of water, a seal had appeared, snapped up the cap and vanished again!

That was the solitary evidence of any underwater activity we were able to detect, and I returned to London. At the Admiralty I settled down to make myself familiar with the reports which had come in during my absence. There was one new weapon in particular which was causing us concern, and I was anxious to know if there had been any developments on it.

The first hint we had of the weapon being used had been in January, 1940. A report came in from the 6,700-ton British merchant ship *Pacific Reliance* that when she was entering the Bristol Channel there had been an explosion within fifty or a hundred yards of her. Fortunately, she suffered no damage.

The ship's position at the time showed that she was in about a hundred fathoms of water, and we knew this to be too deep for mines. Therefore we had to find another explanation. From the evidence, it seemed fairly certain that the *Pacific Reliance* had been attacked by a U-boat which had fired a torpedo at her. But it was not an ordinary torpedo. If that had missed the target it would merely have continued on harmlessly. Here was a torpedo which, even when it missed making a direct strike, still exploded.

The facts seemed to point to only one possible conclusion: the warhead of the torpedo was fitted with a magnetic pistol.

The principle of this particular firing device was well known to the British Navy. Torpedoes fitted with magnetic pistols were used by Swordfish aircraft of the Fleet Air Arm which attacked the Italian battlefleet in its own harbour at Taranto in November, 1940.

Although we did not know the exact nature of the German magnetic pistol, experience with our own type showed that this was not an entirely satisfactory weapon. In theory, it was much more likely to get a kill than the conventional torpedo. When a torpedo is aimed, two factors have to be taken into account: the position of the target vessel and her underwater draft. A torpedo may run with perfect accuracy for direction, but if it is running too deep – say twelve feet down, when the ship at which it is fired draws ten feet – it will pass under the ship's keel without doing any damage. It was to remedy this that the magnetic pistol was fitted. Even if a torpedo were running deep, once it came into the magnetic field of a ship the magnetic pistol would explode it. The damage along the length of a ship's bottom could be very much greater from such an explosion than from a torpedo scoring a direct hit; a direct hit might cause purely localised damage which could be sealed off by closing watertight bulkhead doors.

That, as I say, was the theory. But in practice a magnetic torpedo was not nearly as infallible.

As everyone knows, the earth itself is a vast magnet, with lines of magnetic force running between the two poles. If a torpedo fitted with a magnetic pistol rocked up and down while running shallow it was likely to be affected by the earth's magnetic field which was strong enough to cause it to explode. In the case of the *Pacific Reliance*, we decided, this was what had happened.

By February, a number of similar reports came in of explosions in the vicinity of ships in waters too deep for mining. From these we concluded that German U-boats were regularly using the magnetic pistol on their torpedoes.

The Director of Torpedoes and Mining recommended that all warships and merchantmen should be warned immediately that any unexplained explosion occurring close to them in deep water probably meant that a U-boat was in the vicinity attacking with magnetic torpedoes. We accordingly informed Trade Division and the Vice-Chief of Naval Staff. The warning went out to merchant vessels, but by some oversight this vitally important information was not sent to warships. It was purely by chance that this failure came to light, and not until the very moment when it might have resulted in disastrous consequences.

In April, 1940, Hitler invaded Norway. A British Expeditionary Force was hurriedly mounted and sent to aid the Norwegians. The intention was to land our troops at ports north and south of Trondheim and at Narvik. Admiral of the Fleet Lord Cork and Orrery was given command of the expedition against Narvik.

Lord Cork was in the cruiser *Aurora* escorting the troop transports. Vice-Admiral William J. Whitworth, flying his flag in the battleship *Warspite*, was to cover the landings. He also had a number of destroyers.

Admiral Whitworth knew that there were enemy warships lurking in the Narvik fjords, so before entering he sent in a small probing force of destroyers to reconnoitre. One of them, H.M.S. *Bedouin*, was circling inside Ofot Fjord, which leads to the port of Narvik, when there was an explosion within fifty yards of her.

The previous November, soon after my arrival at the Admiralty, we had issued a questionnaire to all ships. The idea was that if any unexplained underwater explosions occurred, ships were to signal to us in the form of a reply to the questionnaire so that we should be in possession immediately of certain essential facts which would give us some clue to the cause of the explosion. The captain of the *Bedouin* sent his signal.

At DTMI, Captain Maitland-Dougall and I studied the signal and came to our conclusions.

"The depth of the water at that spot is a hundred fathoms – too deep for mines."

"In fact, there's no minefield in the area at all."

"It looks like another of these magnetic torpedoes."

Lord Cork, who had received the report of the explosion, had also realised it could not have been caused by a mine. He signalled to Admiral Whitworth what he believed to be the probable cause, and repeated his signal to the Admiralty. Fortunately, a copy of all messages connected with underwater explosions came to us at DTMI.

The moment that we read that Lord Cork believed the explosion was probably due to a shell fired from an enemy heavy shore battery, we knew there was something very far wrong. It was quite apparent that neither he nor Admiral Whitworth – nor indeed any of the British warships engaged in the operations around Narvik – were aware of the possibility of magnetic torpedoes. It was then that we realised that by an extraordinary oversight on someone's part the warning had never gone out to warships at all. And now the oversight looked as if it might have the most tragic consequences. Lord Cork, in the belief that the explosion was due to a shell fired from a shore battery, had decided how he was going to deal with it. His signal to the Admiralty stated that he proposed to send the *Warspite* into the fjord to reduce the batteries presumed responsible.

"Good Lord!" I said, horrified. "If that was a magnetic torpedo, there's a submarine up the fjord. The *Warspite* will steam straight into a trap."

Maitland-Dougall and I at once took the problem to our Director who ordered me to go to the office of the Vice-Chief of Naval Staff.

"Get round there hotfoot," he said, "and point out the facts."

But it was not as simple as that. Perhaps, in my urgency to make the point, I gave the staff officer to whom I spoke the impression that he should tell Lord Cork not to send the *Warspite* into the fjord.

He said rather stiffly: "There has always been a tradition in the Navy that you leave operations to the man on the spot. You don't interfere from the Admiralty."

And, of course, an excellent tradition this is. It would be quite intolerable for a commander involved in a battle at sea suddenly to have his plans countered by someone hundreds of miles away who could not possibly appreciate the situation as he could on the spot. While accepting this completely, I still had to try to get it over that the *Warspite* might be heading for calamity.

"It's quite contrary to all Naval tradition," said the staff officer, still harping on interference.

Every second that passed worsened the situation. I could visualise the *Warspite* steaming towards the fjord. Once she entered the enclosed, narrow waters, she would be severely restricted in her manoeuvres. She would be a sitting duck for a waiting U-boat.

"It's all very well for you – you're R.N.V.R.," said the staff officer. "We never tell our officers what to do."

This implication of the chasm of difference between the Royal Navy and the Volunteer Reserve was a subject for debate. Possibly, also, this was a suitable place for it. But it was not the time.

"For Heaven's sake," I said, "surely it's your duty to tell the commander on the spot there may be a submarine there. At least, tell him that."

Finally, I achieved my point. It was decided that a signal could be sent which would tactfully give Lord Cork the facts while at the same time complying with the tradition of non-interference. I was too relieved to pay very close attention to the actual wording, but it went something like this: "Admiralty experts consider explosion may be due to magnetic pistol torpedo fired from submarine."

Returning to our office, I waited, wondering whether already it might not be too late for the information sent to serve its purpose. It seemed a very long time before word came through from the forces operating off Narvik. When it did, it was well worth the waiting.

Lord Cork, on receiving the signal, had ordered an asdic sweep – that is a submarine search – of the fjord to be made. The destroyers *Fearless* and *Brazen* went in and swiftly detected a U-boat hidden under the grey surface of the fjord. Depth charges were dropped. The U-boat was sunk.

She proved to be the *U-49*. From her shattered wreck, documents were later salvaged which gave the position of all German U-boats taking part in the invasion of Norway.

Ofot Fjord supplied us with one further success. An unexploded German torpedo was found stranded on the snow-covered shore. Part of it was recovered and sent to us at

DTMI in London. Apart from supplying the final evidence that our deductions on the U-boat's presence had been sound it was something we had long wanted to get our hands on: a German magnetic torpedo pistol.

Chapter 5

A New Danger – The First Acoustic Mine

By a coincidence, my second journey up to Scotland in 1940 also took me aboard H.M.S. *Rodney*. This time, however, instead of being prevented from entering harbour, the battleship was trapped at her anchorage, unable to put to sea. We believed a new underwater weapon was involved, one for which there was no known counter. In fact, during the preceding six weeks or so we had suspected the existence of a new type of mine but we had been unable to establish conclusively its nature.

The first suggestion that we had a new weapon to contend with came towards the end of August when a small Dutch diesel-engined coaster called the *Marne* was mined off the Humber. The circumstances made us suspicious. The explosion was not directly under the ship as it should have been if it had been caused by a magnetic mine.

A few days after the Dutchman was blown up, the cruiser *Galatea* was entering the Humber at twenty knots when there was an explosion about forty yards from her bows. A week later the same thing happened when the *Galatea* was steaming into the Thames Estuary.

We went into the reports on all three explosions minutely. The facts showed that they were typical ground mine explosions. But they were not magnetic mines. If they had been, the chances were that the *Galatea* would not have been so lucky. It looked as if we were faced with a new "secret weapon", a successor to the magnetic mine.

Daily more reports began to flood in of similar types of explosions. These were sent to our technical experts to see what they could make of them. The experts were divided into three separate schools of thought.

The first believed the mystery explosions were due to time bombs dropped by the Luftwaffe. The bombs could have been dumped by aircraft anxious to get back to their bases, possibly because our fighters were on their tails; or they could have been dropped accidentally because crews imagined they were over land at the time. But there was a third possibility: they might have been dropped deliberately in order to mislead us into thinking a shipping channel had been mined. Such a ruse would involve our minesweepers in endless, unproductive work, because they would never succeed in detonating the bombs, but as these would continue to go off it would be necessary to close the affected channels just in case a new kind of mine was involved. This would completely stop merchant shipping movements and put the ports out of action. It might be wondered why the Germans should risk crews and aircraft to do this when they could drop mines instead. The answer to that is simple: shortage of mines. We ourselves were extremely short of mines to drop by aircraft in the early days of the war, and the Germans might be in the same position. (Actually, I put up a suggestion to try to overcome our shortage of airborne mines. It was that our aircraft should fly out loaded with domestic dustbins which they would drop by parachute so that they would be clearly seen before they sank in enemy waters. The fact that something had been dropped would bring the enemy minesweepers into action; the discovery that they had achieved no results would give them the same headache as we had when we encountered the unknown; and even if they recovered any of the dustbins they could not be sure that these were all that had been dropped. The dustbins could have kept a great many enemy ships at a standstill, but whether Operation Dustbin was ever carried out by the R.A.F. I never heard.)

The second school of experts called in to suggest an explanation for the mystery explosions were convinced that these were due to spontaneous detonations by magnetic mines, and it was quite by chance that they had gone off near passing ships.

The third school came up with a most ingenious solution. They believed the mines were of a specially sensitive magnetic type and had gone off as a result of changes in the earth's magnetic field. To back their theory they pointed out that some of the mystery explosions had occurred during magnetic storms. To check this theory we asked Air Ministry wireless and radar experts to find out if there had been a magnetic storm, and what its intensity in gauss (measure of magnetic force) had been, at the time of each succeeding explosion.

Captain Maitland-Dougall and I still kept to our original hunch. We believed that the explosions were due to acoustic mines. But until we had more positive evidence we could not say for sure.

Evidence which seemed to support our theory came from the number of reports received from captains of motor torpedo boats belonging to our Coastal Forces. Several of them said there had been explosions within fifty to a hundred feet of their speeding vessels. The underwater noise and vibration produced by an M.T.B. at speed is pretty considerable. The fact that they should be so frequently involved seemed highly significant.

To see if I could get a first-hand impression of the explosions I went on a couple of scouting expeditions by M.T.B. flotillas from the Coastal Force base at Harwich, appropriately named H.M.S. *Beehive* because of its buzzing M.T.Bs. The first sortie was out towards the Dutch coast, the second to the Thames Estuary. Both were areas where many of the mystery explosions had been reported. But neither trip produced a single bang.

Another type of ship involved in a more than usual number of these explosions were diesel-engined coasters. Again, like the M.T.Bs., they produced considerable underwater noise and vibration. They were not usually as fortunate as the fast M.T.Bs; they suffered many casualties. In fact, so heavy were the losses of one well-known firm of coastal ship owners that the managing director stormed into the Admiralty.

"What the hell is the Navy doing about it?" he demanded.

He was brought to the DTMI Section and handed over to Maitland-Dougall and me. We listened to him until some of his fury had subsided and then told him frankly, though in strict confidence, something of our difficulties and what we were trying to do to overcome them. There was plenty of evidence to show that we had not been idle in our efforts to master the German mines, and when he left the Admiralty I am glad to say his faith in the Royal Navy was considerably restored.

In the middle of our efforts to establish an answer to the problem of the new mine, the great blitz of London began. It started on a gloriously sunny Friday afternoon in September, when nearly four hundred German aircraft bombed Woolwich Arsenal, the docks at Millwall, Limehouse and Rotherhithe, the Surrey Docks and the wharves by Tower Bridge; the City itself, Westminster, Kensington and West Ham. As the fires blazed from the capital that night, the Luftwaffe returned to feed them again and again.

After the long deluge of high-explosive and incendiary bombs, the Germans began to include parachute magnetic mines. Reports streaming in after the "all clear" had been sounded one morning showed that there was a total of no fewer than 150 parachute mines to be made safe. It was then that we were called in. An idea of the magnitude of the task is shown by the fact that there were at that time only two sets of non-magnetic tools available to tackle these delicately deadly mines, one set in the Admiralty at DTMI, and the other in the *Vernon* at Portsmouth; and there were only six Naval officers capable of making mines safe, three of us at DTMI, and three in the *Vernon*.

Manufacture of more non-magnetic tools was put in hand as a top priority job, and there was no shortage of volunteers ready to use them. A crowd of officers and ratings queued up in the *Vernon* to take a hasty instruction course in the ticklish technique of making safe the magnetic mines. Within forty-eight hours there were something like forty R.N.V.R. officers and a number of R.N. petty officers standing by ready to cope with aerial mine bombardment. One of the volunteers who had earlier enrolled at DTMI after having been trained at *Vernon* to render mines safe was a man about sixty named Raphael Saunders. He wore the ribbon of the D.S.O., which I later learned he had won at Zeebrugge.

He came to me and said: "I want a job."

"Do you want to make mines safe?"

"Show me how and I will."

It so happened that when Dick Ryan, the lieutenant-commander with whom I had shared a taxi from Waterloo on my arrival at the Admiralty, went out to render safe some of the magnetic mines he agreed to take Saunders along as his assistant.

Next day when Dick reported before going out to tackle more mines, I asked him who he wanted to take with him. "I'll have Saunders again," he said. At that very moment as they were about to set out together, however, six newly-trained petty officers arrived at the office from *Vernon*. It was our aim, as soon as we had enough people trained, that each team should consist of an officer with a petty officer or rating, so one of the newcomers went out with Dick instead of Saunders.

This proved very fortunate for Saunders. During the morning word came through from Dagenham, where Dick Ryan had gone to deal with a mine, that he and his companion had both been killed.

Although it was always to be expected in this sort of work, the news particularly affected me because I knew both Ryan and his wife well. I asked Captain Maitland Dougall if I might be allowed to go and break the news to Mrs. Ryan, who was in a nursing home in the country awaiting the arrival of a baby.

Maitland-Dougall agreed, and I went off on my sombre journey. On my arrival at the nursing home, Mrs. Ryan said simply:

"I know. I have heard the news."

Her calm courage was most moving. It was a quality she was to need in the days to come, for after the loss of her husband she also lost the baby.

Another officer, Lieutenant Easton, R.N.V.R., of the Land Incident Section, had an extraordinary escape while working on a mine which crashed through the ceiling of a house in London. The rating who was assisting him was not so fortunate.

The magnetic mines which dropped on land were set off by a clockwork fuse mechanism. It ran for twenty seconds, buzzing quite audibly. If you ran fast, the twenty seconds gave just sufficient time to get away if the fuse had the full time to run. But when magnetic mines were parachuted on London, the mechanism had frequently partially run its course before the mines were tackled. So if the mechanism started buzzing while work was going on to make a mine safe, the order was to run as fast and far as possible. In the case of Dick Ryan and his companion, the warning buzz had obviously come too late for them to get away; the explosion had been almost instantaneous.

When Lieutenant Easton and his assistant heard the buzz, they both leapt for the door of the room where they were working, but they became tightly jammed together in the frame. Before they could move, the explosion came. The rating was killed outright; Easton was practically flayed alive by the blast and almost every bone in his body was broken. He spent eighteen months in hospital, and then he returned to duty. He received the George Cross.

One of the *Vernon* officers, Lieutenant Hodges, R.N.V.R., who had been games master at Winchester in civilian life, was within thirty yards when a mine lodged on a bridge across the Thames near Richmond went off; that, I think, was the closest anyone was to one of these explosions and yet remained unscathed. At least, almost unscathed. When he returned to the Admiralty, his clothes were torn, his eyes were bloodshot and he was covered with dust and muck.

His first words – and this gives some idea of the spirit of the man – were: "Where is the next job?"

"No more jobs for you at present," he was told. "You are going in to the sick bay to get some treatment for shock."

What must rank as one of the luckiest escapes of all came about during the rendering safe of a mine which I happened to find.

By this time, my own house in London had been bombed and I had taken a temporary flat in the White House in Albany Street. One morning as I was leaving for the Admiralty, I found on the front steps of the flat a piece of metal which I recognised as part of a magnetic mine. A policeman to whom I spoke said it must have come from an explosion which had occurred in Regent's Park. With the policeman I went over to the park to see the crater.

"Where did the second one go off?" I asked.

"We don't know anything about a second one," said the policeman.

"Well that's odd," I said. "They are always dropped in pairs. Two of these mines make a plane-load."

"We haven't had any reports about another explosion just hereabouts," said the policeman.

"Then there must be another one lying about unexploded."

We went and checked on A.R.P. records. They had a report of an object that had come through the roof of a house in Harrington Square, Camden Town. There was no doubt that it was the twin of the mine that had exploded in Regent's Park.

I phoned through to DTMI to ask for a set of tools to be sent out to me so that I could tackle it, but Maitland-Dougall said:

"Don't you waste your time up there. We have been bombed. We're overwhelmed. You get in straight away, and we'll send someone up to deal with the mine."

At once I hurried to the Admiralty. The walls of our room had been blown out; we were open to the skies. Our records were all over the place, and everything was in terrible confusion. We set to work trying to get things back to order and when night came we continued by the light of fluttering candles.

Meanwhile, Lieutenant Moore, R.N.V.R., a torpedo-man at DTMI, was sent up to Harrington Square accompanied by Lieutenant Perks, R.N.R., who was a master mariner working as our chart expert. They found that the house where the mine had landed was a tall old-fashioned tenement. The tail of the mine was still sticking up through a hole in the roof, and the nose was resting on the gas stove in the kitchen of the top flat.

Moore sized up the situation. If the fuse started running while he was working on the mine, he knew that neither he nor Perks would stand a chance. There would be no time to get down the stairs and out of the house even if the fuse ran the full twenty seconds. The mine would blow up, the whole house would come crashing down on them, and they would be buried beneath it. Fully realising this, Moore still went ahead with the task.

As he unscrewed the fuse, it began to run. He decided that the only course was to go on unscrewing it. He pulled it out of the mine, where its base was in the explosive charge, and hurled it out of the kitchen window. A second after it left his hand, the fuse went off like a hand grenade.

Moore received the George Cross.

The magnetic qualities of the mines had no bearing on their use in the London blitz. They were dropped purely for their enormous destructive power. The mines were bigger than any we had previously handled and contained a thousand kilogrammes of high explosive – about a ton. Since they came down by parachute they did not penetrate the ground but went off with maximum blast effect. One of them blew down no less than six hundred houses.

As so often happened through their indiscriminate use of new weapons, the Germans presented us at DTMI with evidence of two refinements they had introduced into their magnetic mines. These were discovered by Maitland-Dougall while poking about in the debris after one of the mines had gone off. He spotted pieces of mechanism which he recognised as magnetic and unearthed as many as he could. These were assembled, and as a result we discovered that the mine had worked on bi-polar magnetism, which meant that it could be exploded by both North and South polar magnetism, a threat which in future had to be guarded against in degaussing of shipping; and it had also been fitted with a period delay mechanism, dubbed by us a "clicker". The "clicker" made it possible for a magnetic sweep to pass harmlessly over a mine for up to fifteen times before the mine exploded; the mechanism could be set for the mine to go off on any of the fifteen occasions. Thus, if it was set in the seventh position, the magnetic needle of the mine would cause it to go click six times safely, but on the seventh click the mine would explode. With the various combinations possible, the only way to ensure that a channel was safe after mines had been laid was to sweep it fifteen times at least, a formidable burden on the minesweepers. It was a device of the "clicker" type which I had feared might have defied my attempts to ensure Hoy Sound was clear of mines on the occasion I went up to Scapa Flow.

It was early in October that I next went to Scotland. The report which sent me hurrying north suggested that at last I should have the opportunity to tackle an acoustic mine.

The facts were that while a number of ships of the Home Fleet were lying in the Firth of Forth the Luftwaffe made a night raid on the area. Crews of barges flying barrage balloons to protect the ships said they had seen parachute mines dropping on to the anchorage. Two ships of the First Minesweeping Flotilla fitted with the Double-ell sweep made a thorough search but without result. Within a few hours, the Fleet prepared to leave. The destroyers moved off first. But as H.M.S. *Zulu*, a Tribal Class destroyer, was swinging round off Inverkeithing Island near the Forth Bridge there was an explosion ten yards from her stern. The damage was sufficient to put her out of action. As one of the parachute mines had been seen to fall within a hundred and fifty yards of the battleship *Rodney*, the explosion which crippled the *Zulu* caused considerable alarm. At once all movements of the Fleet were stopped.

When I arrived aboard the *Rodney* I met Lieutenant-Commander Lewis, the battleship's torpedo officer, who gave me all the facts he had. Next I visited the balloon barrage vessels and questioned the crews. Finally, after a full day's effort, I pinpointed the position where, from all accounts, the mine appeared to lie. The spot was marked with a dan buoy – a floating spar with a warning flag on it – and I called in a *Vernon* officer to see if he could explode it by dropping depth charges. The anchorage resounded with the reverberations of the exploding depth charges, but the mine refused to react.

Finally, I said to Lewis: "There's only one thing left to do. I will get a trawler and we'll try running over the spot at full speed. The mine might be fitted with some form of period delay mechanism (that is a 'clicker')."

The crew of a drifter volunteered for the experiment. We reduced their number to the bare minimum needed to work the vessel, and all hands were warned that when we approached the danger spot they must keep their feet and legs off the deck as much as possible by hanging on to rigging or other handgrips. If they stood on deck, the shock effect from a mine explosion would be enough to hurl them off their feet, possibly enough to break a leg. (When H.M.S. *Nelson* had been mined, many casualties occurred in the 'tween decks; men were rattled like peas in a can between deck and deckhead and injuries were mostly broken legs or concussion.)

We set off across the grey, sullen waters of the Firth. For myself I devoutly hoped that if we succeeded in blowing up the mine we should all come down in one piece.

With her engines turning at maximum revolutions, the drifter steamed across the patch of water marked by the spar. Nothing happened.

We went back and carried out a series of agitated manoeuvres, first full ahead, then full astern, to make maximum vibrations. Again and again we churned over the spot, water boiling under our stern. But still nothing happened.

For all our sonic prodding, we could produce no result. I called off the attempt.

"The thing must be a dud," I decided.

With considerable relief, the drifter crew took their vessel back to base and I returned aboard the *Rodney*. Lewis and I reported to the captain that we believed the mine had somehow become ineffective and that the flagship could be safely moved. But, just in case there was a delayed-action kick left in the mine, it would be prudent to move the ship as slowly and quietly as possible.

The smaller escort ships cautiously put to sea first, and then the *Rodney's* anchor chain was hauled in gingerly. First the battleship went gently astern, and then, slowly and with infinite care, her bows were swung round until they pointed down the Forth. With scarcely a ripple at her counter, the vast bulk of the flagship glided seaward to join her escort.

At the request of the captain I remained on board during this time.

The first part of the task, to ensure that the Fleet proceeded safely to sea, had been accomplished; but the second – to solve the mystery of the mine – had not been achieved. We still did not know whether in fact the enemy's new mine was acoustic.

On my return to London, I had a telephone call from Plymouth. It was Captain Hodson, the Minesweeping Captain with whom I had worked on the magnetic mines off Falmouth. Now he had a problem on his hands at Devonport.

He said: "An enemy aircraft has dropped a mine in the dockyard at the entrance to Number Eight Basin. It's completely blocking the entrance, and the *Renown's* inside – I can't get her out."

This was serious: obviously, the battle-cruiser would have to stay locked up in the basin until they got rid of the mine.

"We've tried the magnetic sweep," said Hodson, "but it's no go. Nothing's happened."

"It's probably an acoustic mine," I said.

I told him of the *Rodney's* mine and described our attempts to blow it up by steaming a trawler over it.

I'll have a go at that," said Hodson.

"For heaven's sake be careful," I said. It was rather a stupid thing to say. In this work there was a certain point only to which care was really of any consequence; after that it was luck alone that decided. But we always told each other to be careful when trying anything new.

Hodson was an elderly man, and he would have been perfectly justified in turning over the job to someone younger, but that was not his way. He immediately called for a volunteer crew and embarked in a minesweeping trawler.

He carried out the same manoeuvres as we had followed in the Firth of Forth, but his efforts were more fruitful. The mine exploded, blowing up the trawler. Unfortunately, several of the crew were killed, but Hodson was among the survivors picked up out of the water.

When he came out of hospital after a day or two, I telephoned him to say how sorry I was to hear he had been blown up.

"You've nothing to be sorry about," he said. "I'm only delighted we got rid of that mine."

It was the typical reaction of a minesweeping captain. Their job was to keep the channels open. Whatever the cost, that was what they always worked to achieve.

The Devonport experiment had cost the lives of men and the loss of a ship, but it had cleared the entrance to the basin so that the *Renown* could put to sea; it had also supplied the proof that we had awaited: now we knew beyond doubt that the new weapon was an acoustic mine.

Knowing that the mine worked on the acoustic principle was one thing, but dealing with it was quite another. Scientists were experimenting to produce a counter measure in the form of a device which made a noise underwater. But they were working largely in the dark, and until they knew precisely how the mine was detonated their efforts might be very wide of success. The only way to make sure was to recover the mine intact and discover exactly how it functioned.

From casualty reports it began to look as though a crop of acoustic mines had been dropped in the Bristol Channel area. Several of us at DTMI set off to try our luck around the South Wales coast. While I was down there word came through on October 29th that two mines had been dropped near some railway lines during a raid on Newport.

At once I told my driver to make for Newport as fast as he could. We had a mines disposal car, a big, powerful vehicle, red-painted at the front and fitted with a warning bell like a police car so that it could charge through traffic. We made Newport in good time and called in at the police headquarters to find just where the mines lay. A senior police officer said he would come along to show us. We drove to a vacant lot, along one side of which ran a railway embankment, and stopped the car. The police officer pointed across the waste ground. Two hundred yards away lay two large metal cylinders with parachutes attached. They were mines all right.

I prepared to make a wary approach. As I did so, I heard the noise of a shunting engine operating somewhere along the railway line at the top of the embankment.

We had no warning. The explosions came with such suddenness that we were too stunned even to throw ourselves flat on the ground. All that we were aware of was noise battering our ears and, in the fraction of a second before our eyes instinctively closed, the whole stretch of waste land seemed to be erupting skywards.

When the debris settled, both mines were gone. I went over and inspected the craters, which were something like a hundred yards across. Presently the sound of shunting operations sounded along the railway line. It was this, the vibration starting the bomb fuses, which had detonated the mines, destroying the evidence we had waited so long to obtain. However, if the mines had to be destroyed by this means, it was at least comforting that it should have happened while we were still a safe two hundred yards away and not a few seconds later when we should have been too close to know anything about it.

In the mine craters I found some pieces of casing and a tail cone bearing the letters *Ld*. The markings on the cone were strange to us and with other fragments I gathered indicated a new type of mine mechanism.

I telephoned Maitland-Dougall at the Admiralty and gave him the information so that he could pass it on to all mines disposal officers. If they came across a mine bearing the letters *Ld* they would know they had to tackle a new type. The facts collected would also be reported to the various intelligence branches of the Services to see what they could make of them. It might be that they would be able to identify the factory in Germany at which a certain part had been made and, if priority justified it, the factory would become the target of a bombing raid. Some idea of the exhaustive way that information of this kind was followed up and acted on is shown by a discovery made at the time the first magnetic mine was recovered at Shoeburyness. On being dropped from its carrier aircraft, the tail cone of a mine became detached and acted like a drogue, pulling out the parachute by means of stout cords. These cords were recovered from the Shoeburyness mines and sent to experts. On analysis, the cords proved to have been made from hemp grown in Yugoslavia. As a result of this information the Ministry of Economic Warfare set about buying up the entire Yugoslav hemp crop to deprive Germany of this source.

Maitland-Dougall also had news for me. He had just received a report that a mine had been found in the bed of the River Ogmore at Barry. I hurried off to cover the twenty-odd miles by car hoping to get there before some everyday piece of local noise-making blasted this latest piece of evidence sky high. It occurred to me that as the next day was my birthday that might bring me luck. However, by the time I got there a party of locally-based R.M.S.O.s – Rendering Mines Safe Officers – had beaten me to it. They were ready to go to work. The following day one of them, Lieutenant Cummings,

R.N.V.R., made the mine safe, and it was sent to H.M.S. *Vernon* for dissecting.

When the report on its workings came through, we realised how extraordinarily lucky Cummings had been. The acoustic mine was one of the trickiest weapons we had encountered. Once it fell into sixteen feet or more of water it armed itself. After that it was a death trap. The mere scraping of a screwdriver on the outer casing was enough to explode it. The Ogmore River mine had fallen into water, but fortunately for Cummings not the fatal depth needed to arm it. For his successful handling of this very hazardous task he received the George Medal.

The report from *Vernon* also showed that the mine was fitted with a most effective device to defy counter-measures being used against it. The use of depth charges, which we had tried in the Firth of Forth, would never have detonated the mine. Its acoustic unit was devised to pick up the sound of a ship at some distance and to be operated only as the sound gradually built up to a crescendo – in effect, to distinguish between conventional ship noises and the more explosive noises which might be used in an attempt to get rid of it. The acoustic unit responded to a sound vibration of 230 cycles per second. This was unexpected; a frequency in the thousands had been anticipated.

A week later a second acoustic mine was recovered at Birchington, Kent, and its frequency confirmed that the first was no fluke.

Now the scientists had the knowledge to make an effective counter-measure. It worked on the same principle as a road drill and was called a Kango Hammer. Initially, it was fitted to the flooded fore-peak of a minesweeping trawler, but later it was found to work better rigged on the outside of the hull of a sweeping vessel.

All went well with this method until the following July when an acoustic mine recovered on the Norfolk coast was found to have a refinement. It worked on the original frequency, but it had been fitted with a period delay mechanism so that it could be made active as many as twelve times before it exploded. A counter-measure had to be found to deal with this.

Quite a long while after we had solved the problem of the acoustic mine, there was a strange and unexpected sequel. It involved the most unlikely vessel – a Thames sailing barge. The barge had been sailing in company with one of her sisters across some sandbanks close to the Essex coast when she was blown up.

When the report of this loss came to us at DTMI, we were rather alarmed. The barges are usually of all wood construction and there is not enough metal in their fittings and gear to detonate a magnetic mine. Moreover, the one which had been blown up was carrying a cargo of shingle, and there was certainly nothing magnetic about that. The question that arose was whether the Germans had devised some entirely new type of mine which could be touched off by any kind of ship.

To try to find out, I set off on a trip in the barge which escaped destruction when the explosion occurred. We sailed from Erith to work our way down the Thames to Gravesend. The Thames barges, among the last of our sailing vessels, are unfortunately a rare sight these days on the London River, for they are among the loveliest working ships devised by man. They are also among the most economical. The one I sailed in carried the usual crew of a man and a boy, but the gear to handle the great ochre spritsail, the topsail and gib, is ingenious. The skipper and boy could manage their craft perfectly well.

With the skipper at the wheel and the water chuckling under our bows we made our leisurely way downstream. Gradually, I became aware of a noise which sounded quite loud over the hiss and bubble of water flowing past the barge's sides: it was the great barn-door of a rudder chattering and shuddering on its pintles. A suspicion crept into my mind, and I asked the skipper to lower the leeboards. These are fitted one on either side and serve to give lateral resistance, as the barge is a flat-bottomed craft of shallow draft. When the leeboards went down into the water, they too chattered and shuddered as we went through the water.

It was not the surface noise made by the shaking rudder and leeboards which was the trouble. But there was no doubt in my mind that these sounds set up an underwater vibration of a frequency and intensity sufficient to detonate an acoustic mine.

And so the warning went out from the Admiralty to all barge owners that they should tighten up rudders and leeboards in order to prevent the noise. They were also warned that the age-old practice of barge skippers to take short cuts across sandbanks was particularly dangerous because of the large number of acoustic mines liable to be lying in shoal waters – a barge might even run into one of them! The consequence of that would be just as final as would the setting up of the noise necessary to explode the mine. In fact, the merest brush, by the barge's hull would be enough to cause an explosion.

Just how sensitive the German, acoustic mine was is shown by the experience of Lieutenant J.S. Mould of the Royal Australian Naval Volunteer Reserve, who later won both the George Medal and the George Cross for his work in making mines safe. He was sent to recover an acoustic mine which had been uncovered by the tide along the east coast. As he approached the mine, he saw a crab crawling on to the casing. He was 250 yards away, and he decided to lie flat on the sand and watch what happened. It was as well that he did. The crab struggled up on to the mine and scuttled across the casing. The mine blew up with a shattering roar!

Chapter 6

Luck Assists but Death Strikes

The more we learned from our investigations into the secrets of the German underwater weapons, the more convinced we were at DTMI that any single type which the enemy had evolved could well have lost Britain the war if ways had not been found to deal with it. It was providential, therefore, that the Royal Navy succeeded in mastering each of them in turn. But, looking back now, the most sobering thought of all is the extraordinary part that chance played in our success. If events had not worked out quite as they did when the enemy sprang some new piece of ingenuity, it is impossible to say just what the consequences might have been. What is certain is that we had our share of luck.

The discovery of the secrets of the German T-type magnetic mine is a case in point. A stroke of sheer good fortune presented us with the facts about this weapon. All the facts, that is to say, except those relating to one possible modification. Unfortunately, before we were able to learn the details of the one outstanding but vital piece of information, it was to cost the life of one of our best and most experienced officers.

Our initial good fortune over the T-type mine came about as a result of the action of a chief petty officer, a resourceful and quick-witted man. He was serving in an escort destroyer in the North Sea early in 1940. The destroyer detected a U-boat on her asdic and attacked with depth charges. The U-boat frantically twisted and weaved to throw off her pursuer, but eventually, badly damaged, she was forced to surface. Her crew swarmed up from below and dived overboard to swim towards the destroyer which they could see swiftly bearing down on them. A moment or two after they had taken to the sea, a solitary figure in officer's uniform was sighted emerging from the U-boat's conning tower. Obviously, he was the captain and equally clear was the reason why he had waited a few seconds after the others had gone: he had been firing the scuttling charges. So very shortly the U-boat would go to the bottom, and there was nothing that could stop it.

All this had been seen by the chief petty officer standing on the fo'c'sle of the approaching destroyer. But he had noted something further. None of the Germans who had emerged from the submarine had been seen to throw overboard the confidential books. The ship's papers and confidential books, therefore, were still on board. The Germans were depending on the U-boat sinking swiftly enough to take the books safely to the bottom before anyone could possibly get hold of them.

By this time, the destroyer had come right alongside the foundering submarine. The chief petty officer did not hesitate. He swung himself over the fo'c'sle rail of the destroyer and dropped down on to the submarine's conning tower. In a flash he vanished through the open conning-tower hatch.

Down in the deserted control room, as he had expected, books and papers lay in confusion where they had been hurriedly abandoned by the German crew. He grabbed an armful of these, sprang for the ladder and a moment or two later reappeared through the conning-tower hatch. From there he leapt just in time across the dividing space between the sinking U-boat and the destroyer's rail.

For his initiative and courage he was properly decorated.

Among the documents which by his presence of mind he had saved from going to the bottom with the doomed submarine was an official German handbook which appeared to deal with mines. It was passed to us at DTMI, and immediately we asked the Director of Naval Intelligence to have it translated. As soon as we knew the contents, we realised the importance of our acquisition, for the book was a manual of instruction issued by the German Admiralty on the use of a new type of submarine-laid magnetic mine.

From the pages of the German manual we learned that the mine was seven feet, seven inches long and had a diameter of twenty-one inches; its explosive charge weighed 1,220 pounds. There were two types of the mine, and detailed diagrams of each were given. One unusual feature was that an anchor and cable were fitted to the nose so that the mine could be moored in position. We surmised that the reason for this was that the mine was intended to be laid in deeper water than was usual for the normal magnetic mine. In order that the minelaying submarine should have time to get clear of the area, a delayed-action device was fitted to the mooring apparatus, and there was also some additional clockwork mechanism which could be pre-set to delay the mine from arming itself for any period up to twelve hours in settings of fifteen minutes each. The magnetic firing unit was similar to that fitted in the aircraft-laid magnetic mines with which we were now familiar, and so the submarine-laid magnetic mine could be swept in the same way.

So far all was highly satisfactory. However, the manual also mentioned that one version of the mine could be fitted with what we called a P.S.E. – the abbreviation for "Prevent Stripping Equipment", officialese for booby trap. The P.S.E. would hinder attempts to make the mine safe. For the information of U-boat commanders and those handling the mines in dockyards, said the manual, such mines would be indicated by a red strip six inches long painted on the outside of the shell of the casing. The nature of the booby trap and its position in the mine were not given. These, then, were the missing facts on the T-type mine.

From the information we had, the experts at H.M.S. *Vernon* were able to work out a detailed drill for making safe the T-type mine. It was the first time this had been possible without actually recovering a mine. We were naturally extremely grateful to the chief petty officer who had risked his life going down into the sinking U-boat to recover the manual.

It was not until July 16, 1941, that the first opportunity occurred to recover one of these mines for dissection. It was washed ashore near Portland and made safe by Lieutenant Edward Tewson, R.N.V.R., one of the mine experts in DTMI, later given the George Medal. It had no booby trap.

On April 14, 1942, H.M.S. *Basset*, a Fleet minesweeper working off Lowestoft, reported sighting a floating object which her captain thought to be a new type of mine. Captain Maitland-Dougall happened to be on leave at the time, and so I had to decide what must be done about it. As Tewson was working on a stranded mine at Brightlingsea, I asked him to go down to Lowestoft to recover and examine the mine reported by the *Basset*.

When Tewson got on board the minesweeper, a Force 6 wind had sprung up and there was a nasty sea running. This made any effort to get near the mine most unpleasant, but Tewson still put off in a boat from the *Basset*. He managed to get close enough to touch the mine, but wind and sea made its immediate recovery impossible. He marked its position with a lighted dan buoy and stood by in the sweeper alongside it until an approaching convoy had passed safely.

The mine was floating in an area which came under the Commander-in-Chief, The Nore, and he demanded that it should be destroyed immediately. Understandably, he was concerned only for the safety of the merchant shipping in that stretch of the North Sea for which he was responsible. But we wanted the mine intact. It was of the T-type and might contain a booby trap or possibly a new magnetic unit. This was something we must attempt to master. There was an interchange of signals between the Admiralty and the Commander-in-Chief, and finally he was persuaded to allow Tewson to stand by the mine throughout the night. Next morning wind and sea had moderated sufficiently for Tewson to rope the mine safely and get it towed ashore.

An R.M.S. party from *Vernon* arrived to help him, and the mine was made safe by Lieutenant Robert Nixon, R.N.V.R. To Nixon's relief it was a straight T-type mine with no booby trap.

It did not, therefore, solve our problem, but it was nevertheless a valuable trophy. Since only one sample of the mine had been recovered, and that nearly a year before, the new mine was sent off by road to Portsmouth to undergo expert scrutiny at *Vernon*.

One day a few months later I had a telephone call from Lieutenant-Commander Edwards, R.N., who was the R.M.S.O. at Yarmouth. He said he had managed to get ashore a T-type mine which had been floating off Corton Sands, and he was now proposing to disarm it.

"Hold the line, will you?" I said, and repeated what he had told me to Maitland-Dougall.

Maitland-Dougall took the receiver from me and said: "Look here, Edwards, are you sure you can tackle this thing?"

Confidently, Edwards gave his assurance that he could.

"I'd rather you didn't," said Maitland-Dougall.

Edwards protested that he had read the captured German manual about the T-type mine and he had also received instruction on how to deal with it during a course he had taken in the *Vernon*.

Maitland-Dougall continued to demur, and finally said: "I'm going to send a *Vernon* officer up to deal with it."

The officer designated was John Mould, the Australian Naval Volunteer Reservist, who was told to come up from *Vernon* to London for briefing, and then he would be sent on to Lowestoft to disarm the Corton mine.

Edwards had to be content with that. I knew how he must be feeling, and I could sympathise with him. The mine was in his area, and he felt it a matter of personal pride that he should be given the chance to tackle it. He was a most experienced officer, and he had disarmed no less than 180 mines of varying types for which he had been awarded the Distinguished Service Cross. But mostly they had been the conventional horned mines, and his experience with magnetic mines was not very great. On the odd occasion when a magnetic parachute mine had dropped in his area, either Dick Ryan or a *Vernon* officer had gone up to deal with it. In fact, it was in

Edwards' company that Dick Ryan had one of his most alarming experiences. It was in the spring of 1940 when he went up to Clacton to investigate an explosion which had blown down a large number of houses. He decided, after inspecting the crater, that there was no doubt that a parachute mine was the cause. But parachute mines were always dropped in pairs, and there had been no report of another similar explosion nor had there been a report of an unexploded mine having fallen.

This was very puzzling, so Ryan went to an A.R.P. warden to see if he could learn anything from him. All the warden could tell him was that it must have been a tremendous explosion which had destroyed the houses because it had blown a *water tank* clean out of one of them and sent it flying a full two hundred yards beyond the area of damage. Ryan asked where the tank was, and the warden led him and Edwards to it. When they reached the spot they found a crowd of local children having a great time clambering up on to the "tank" and jumping off it. But the terrifying part was that it was not a water tank at all: it was the second of the parachute mines which had been dropped. Ryan and Edwards sent the children well away, cleared the area and disarmed the mine. This turned out to be a new type of magnetic mine materially different from the first ones recovered.

While I sympathised with Edwards, whom I knew well and held in high regard professionally, I agreed with Maitland-Dougall that in this particular case it was best to leave the mine to John Mould. However, Edwards thought differently. A short while after he was on the telephone again repeating his request for permission to deal with the mine himself. He said it was likely to become a nuisance now because the area of beach where it lay would have to be roped off and guarded until Mould could arrive.

Maitland-Dougall again refused. He was not at all convinced that Edwards thoroughly understood what he might be up against, and it was a matter of principle with him never to let anyone take unnecessary risks. Edwards was so insistent, though, that Maitland-Dougall finally relented and grudgingly gave his permission to go ahead.

"But do be careful," was his final warning.

A few hours later there was a further telephone call from Lowestoft. This time the caller was the Naval Officer-in-Charge with the tragic news that Edwards was dead. He and a young American naval officer who had been working with him under training, Ensign John Howard, had both been blown to pieces on Corton Sands. Although America was not yet in the war, we were already, at the request of the United States Naval Attaché, training American officers to deal with mines.

Within a matter of minutes of our receiving this news, John Mould arrived at our office from *Vernon*. Maitland-Dougall sent the pair of us off to investigate the disaster. On our arrival at Lowestoft, we reported to Commander Theobald, the Minesweeping Commander, who took us to the melancholy spot where Edwards and his companion had been killed.

Theobald said: "I was watching Edwards at work right till a few seconds before the blast."

But he could not say what Edwards and his companion had been doing at the precise moment of the explosion. This was what I had to try to establish, for it would tell us on what part of the mine they were working when the explosion occurred and, therefore, where the danger was to be apprehended. It was the last few seconds alone that were so vitally important from my point of view in trying to decide what had caused the mine to explode.

We could learn nothing at all from the scene of the tragedy. A huge gash had been torn in the sands where the mine had exploded. Fragments of mine casing, shreds of clothing and human flesh were widely scattered. In one spot lay a severed hand. But of the sequence of events which led to this devastation there was no trace of a clue.

And then, quite unexpectedly, we found an eye-witness. Up on the cliffs and some distance along from where the blast occurred was a coastguard station. A coastguard named

Maitland had been on duty when Edwards and John Howard arrived to deal with the mine. As he had been naturally curious to see how they would go about their task, he turned his telescope on them. He had kept them under observation right until the fatal moment.

We had a photograph of the T-type mine and we showed this to Maitland, asking him to tell us in as much detail as he could recall exactly what had happened. His work had trained him to observe, and he made a very fair job of his reconstruction of the scene he had watched.

"They were working at this end," he said, pointing to the blunt end of the mine in the photograph. We knew this was where the arming clock was situated.

Edwards had apparently taken off the outer cap of the mechanism plate of the mine and then began to work on a small plate. He had removed the securing nuts of this plate, but then he appeared to have experienced some difficulty. Maitland, turning his attention to the young American, had noticed that he was shaping a piece of wood as if to make a wedge for some purpose. Edwards had then begun to hammer what looked to Maitland to be a screwdriver into the mine as if to try to force free the plate he had unscrewed. At that moment the mine blew up.

From the diagram of the T-type mine in the captured German handbook, we could see that the arming clock lay behind the plate which Edwards had been trying to remove. It was therefore apparent that the booby trap was fitted to the arming clock.

Mould and I collected as many fragments of the mine as we could find on the beach and cliff face, and a naval search party scoured the area round about for any that might have been overlooked. From our inspection of these pieces, and by putting them together as far as we were able, we were satisfied that there had been a booby trap. The recovered fragments were sent to *Vernon* to see if there was anything more that the experts down there could make of them.

Sadly we went back to Theobald's office to collate our findings and make arrangements for our journey back to London. While we were in the office a signal arrived reporting that another T-type mine had been seen floating some miles offshore, apparently from the same minefield as the previous one.

Mould and I decided that we must get this new mine. Theobald had standing by a hundred-foot patrol service and minesweeping motor launch which he said we were welcome to use. We signalled our intentions to the DTMI Section at the Admiralty and asked that a van and recovery party from *Vernon* should be sent up to Lowestoft at once. In a few minutes we were hurrying down the jetty to board the launch.

There was a heavy sea running when we left harbour, and as we approached the spot where the mine had been reported we could see its menacing shape rising and falling in the waves. It was clear that we were not going to make an easy capture.

The launch's small dinghy was lowered, and Mould and Petty Officer Polkinghorne, the coxswain of the launch, got down into the boat and pushed off. Polkinghorne handled the bucking dinghy skilfully, keeping the boat close enough for Mould to try to reach the mine from the sternsheets, yet at the same time preventing it from colliding with the mine. In the sea running at the time this was far from easy. It took seamanship and nerve.

While the pair of them battled away, the launch circled them slowly, keeping a cable's length away. Lieutenant Walker, R.N.V.R., who commanded the launch, and I stayed on the bridge to supervise the operation, but in case the mine blew up the deck was cleared of all crew except those strictly necessary to work the ship.

Finally, hanging over the transom of the wildly tossing dinghy, Mould managed to attach a line by means of a clip hook to the mine mooring wire. The dinghy came back and was left on her painter astern of the launch. A stout grassline was made fast to the clip rope securing the mine and carefully paid out for some two hundred and fifty yards of its length. We were taking no chances in case the mine was detonated by the buffeting it would receive from the waves as soon as the towline tightened, nor did we want to risk its coming within the ship's own magnetic field. Slowly we headed towards Corton beach.

When the launch had gone as close inshore as her draught would allow, the towline was transferred to a small motor boat, *Wings of the Morning*, commanded by one of Theobald's officers. The motor boat towed in the mine as far as she could without grounding, and then Mould and Polkinghorne in the dinghy took over for the final stage. Handling the dinghy in the heavy breakers was no easy feat, but they passed the grassline to a party of sailors waiting on the beach to haul the mine ashore, and they beached the dinghy. As soon as we saw them land safely, we headed back to Lowestoft in the launch.

Walker, the launch's captain, had his car standing by, and he drove me to Corton. Once on the beach we found the shore party were having considerable trouble with our catch. A *cheval de frise* of steel scaffolding had been erected below the tide line to serve as an anti-invasion obstacle. At intervals along this barricade, gaps about ten yards wide had been left to enable fishermen to beach their boats. The shore party were trying to drag the mine through one of these gaps. But a strong cross tide had swept the mine northwards so that the line had fouled the groynes and also the steel scaffolding.

We decided to abandon this attempt and to tow the mine by the motor boat about a mile farther along the coast where it could be hauled ashore from a point on the cliffs which faced that part of the beach. The advantage of having the recovering party up on the cliffs was that if the mine should explode during the dragging operation they would be a safe distance away from the blast.

But no sooner had we reached the new landing place than we found ourselves confronted with a fresh danger. The beach and cliff behind it at this spot had been sown with pressure mines by the Army as part of their anti-invasion defences.

When we asked for this area to be temporarily cleared, we were blandly informed by the local Army authorities:

"We have no idea of the exact location of our minefield. All we can advise you to do is to avoid all mounds."

Risking our lives to try to disarm an enemy mine was one thing, but being blown up on our own anti-invasion mines while doing so appeared to be an entirely unnecessary hazard. However, there was nothing to do about it but to keep the beach party as small as possible to lessen the chance of casualties. So we limited those on the beach to Commander Theobald, Mould and myself, Walker and two ratings. The rest of the party under another officer took up position on the cliff top. Treading gingerly in case there were mines underfoot, we handed the towing warp to the party on the cliff and they began once more to haul the mine ashore.

As soon as they got it into the shallows, I waded out to examine it for markings in case it should blow up once it started bumping over the shingle. I wanted at least to be sure of any external evidence it might offer. The casing was heavily encrusted with barnacles and marine growths and crawling with sea lice. The sight of these repellent creatures filled me with violent nausea. I managed, with the mine bumping up and down in the water and my bare hands and sea water, to wash off some of the accumulated filth round the mechanism plate. One result of this was to cut my hands very badly, but the other was the discovery that, on the pitted metal, was painted a six-inch long red strip. The mine was booby-trapped.

After another hour's strenuous tug-of-war, the mine was finally hauled up the beach until it lay clear of the high-water mark. More of the sea growths festooning it were scrubbed off, and we examined the outside shell thoroughly, making a careful note of all markings and lettering.

By then, Lieutenant Armitage had arrived with the recovery party from *Vernon*. He had brought with him a supply of radium and photographic plates.

On either side of the blunt end of the mine opposite the mechanism plate we stuck pieces of stick into the beach and made a small platform on top of each set of sticks. On one platform we placed the radium, on the other a photographic plate. The result from this rather rough and ready X-ray was a shadowy picture on the plate of the internal components of the mine. But, when compared with the diagram in the captured German handbook dealing with the T-type mine, the photograph we had was clear enough to show that the mine had been fitted with the additional item of a booby trap. It was in exactly the position we had expected it to be from the coastguard's observations of the last fatal move made by poor Edwards.

Fully forewarned, we were able to follow the drill laid down for disarming a mine suspected of containing a booby trap. The rest of the job of rendering the mine safe was left to Lieutenant Armitage to complete.

At last we had completed the record on the T-type magnetic mine started for us by the chief petty officer who snatched the handbook from the sinking German U-boat. But for us the triumph was marred by the deaths of Edwards and his young American companion. What might have been a bloodless victory had cost two brave men their lives.

Chapter 7

We Discover a New Mine

It was always most satisfying to us in DTMI when the Germans themselves unwittingly informed us about their new weapons, particularly when they did so well in advance of their use. In our role as detectives, it helped enormously to know what to expect; it put us rather in the position of police who are told by a gang of safe-breakers how they propose to raid a bank. We were able to make effective preparations to deal with the threat instead of finding ourselves, quite unsuspecting, confronted with the reality.

One link with the Germans was through the interrogation centre at Trent Park, Cockfosters, Middlesex, where all enemy prisoners-of-war were taken on their arrival in this country. Sir Philip Sassoon, always a most hospitable host, owned Trent Park, and there, in peace time, had entertained half the British aristocracy. King Edward VIII had played golf over the course laid out in the park. The hospitality offered by the interrogators to the newly-arrived prisoners-of-war had to match the changed nature of the place, which was now festooned with barbed wire, and the altered circumstances of the occasion, but they were not indifferent hosts: they were relaxed and understanding, their manner was sympathetic, they were patient and most attentive listeners. It was through these men that we received so much information about the latest German activities.

The German prisoners, naturally, did not generally realise they had in fact given information of any particular significance. The atmosphere at Cockfosters was very different from the rather rough reception their own propaganda had led them to expect, and the attitude of the interrogators was designed to make them drop their guard and lead to their speaking more freely than they realised. Inevitably, as the conversation was guided skilfully in directions that the interrogators particularly wished to explore, the prisoners unwittingly let out facts which we found interesting and useful.

In order to cover the whole range of intelligence requirements, interrogators had to be acquainted with all sorts of aspects of the war. They were an extremely well-informed group of men. They were, furthermore, very clever psychologists. They were masters of the innocent question, quite remote apparently from anything of military importance, which was capable of producing the highly significant answer.

On occasion, the interrogators did not even have to guide a new arrival into committing indiscretions. Some of them seemed determined to do this without any assistance. They were so filled with conceit and arrogance that they just could not help making fools of themselves. It was a consequence their country had to pay for having allowed itself to be persuaded by a madman that it was peopled by a master race.

After interviewing a Luftwaffe pilot during March, 1941, one of the R.A.F. interrogators telephoned me and recounted what had happened at the interview.

The German pilot had refused to stand to attention or to obey orders. He was completely arrogant.

"I order you to stand to attention," the interrogator had said.

"I am not going to obey you. You are going to be finished in a few weeks."

"What makes you so sure?"

"We have the assurance of the Reichsmarschall Goering that we have a new weapon that will wipe your fleet off the seas and finish you off in six weeks."

As the interrogator repeated this conversation to me, I said: "That sounds formidable. Did he say what the weapon was?"

"According to this chap, it is another type of mine. He claims it will totally destroy our Merchant Fleet – and that we cannot sweep it."

"Can you," I said, "get anything more definite out of him, any precise idea about the nature of the weapon?"

"We've tried," said the interrogator, "but the most we can get is that it's an infinitely superior magnetic mine. If the chap's telling the truth, and Goering has been going around addressing the Luftwaffe about it, it certainly sounds as if it's something out of the ordinary."

He promised to let me know immediately if they discovered any further details. We waited, wondering what we might be up against this time. There was always the possibility that we were being treated to a dose of enemy propaganda, but our instinct was to treat the information as hard fact until it was proved otherwise. It was too serious a possibility to be dismissed merely as idle boasting by the Luftwaffe man. We knew that now the R.A.F. interrogators were on to the investigation they would not let go until they had established it as fact or completely demolished the whole thing as the fantasy of a fanatic.

It did not take them long to establish it as fact. Within a week or so, our friend from Cockfosters came in over the telephone with an important addition to the original story obtained from a second prisoner.

"He says that the designation of the new weapon is the BM 1000," said the interrogator.

This was something definite on which at least we could start to surmise. Our guess was that the number meant that the weight of the charge would be one thousand kilogrammes, near enough a ton. We assumed that the weight and dimensions would be governed by the fact that the weapon would have to fit into the existing mine racks in the aircraft of the special Luftwaffe squadrons trained for mine-laying. From this we could presume that its measurements would be similar to the airborne magnetic mines, that is, six-feet-two long and twenty-four inches in diameter.

For a while the letters *BM* kept us guessing until we decided they must stand for *Bombemine,* a dual purpose bomb and mine. Confirmation of this surmise came shortly after the arrival of another talkative Luftwaffe pilot at Cockfosters.

"He says that the BM 1000 is dropped without a parachute," said the interrogator.

Parachutes prevented accurate aim being achieved, and the bomb-mine had to be capable of being delivered with the same accuracy as was possible with the ordinary aerial bomb.

By mid-April we had a fairly clear picture of what we were up against: a weapon shaped like a bomb and of much the same dimensions as the large magnetic mine and the "Hermann" one-thousand-kilogramme bomb.

The R.A.F. interrogators were now as determined to gather every conceivable fact on the BM 1000 as we were anxious to receive it. From yet another Luftwaffe pilot they had extracted a final piece of information, and suddenly the picture assumed a much more ominous aspect.

"According to German experts," said the voice from Cockfosters, "their new weapon cannot be recovered."

This could only mean one thing: it contained one or more booby traps.

We were not really surprised to learn that the new weapon would be devised to defy all efforts to disarm it. It was the inevitable reaction by the enemy to the very considerable success which had been achieved in breaking down, one after the other, each new weapon they had produced and evolving an effective counter-measure to it. They had convinced themselves at the outset that in the magnetic mine they had a weapon which would win the war. They had boasted this would be so. They had been proved wrong. All their ingenuity – and technically they were brilliantly ingenious – had not so far enabled them to achieve an insoluble threat to our shipping and therefore to our continued existence.

We knew that the Germans were prepared to go to extreme lengths to try to prevent the secrets of their underwater weapons from being discovered: bitter experience had taught us this. From the moment the first magnetic mines were recovered by the Royal Navy, the Germans made up their minds to introduce a new kind of magnetic mine. In doing so, they decided that the new weapon should be of such a nature that in their efforts to recover it as many British mine experts should lose their lives as possible.

It fell to Lieutenant-Commander Glennie, who had been in Ouvry's party at the rendering safe of the first magnetic mines at Shoeburyness, to meet the first mine fitted with a booby trap. He had carried out the usual drill to make the mine safe and took it back with him to H.M.S. *Vernon* for the usual dissection. He was in the mining shed when it was being stripped down. A petty officer unscrewed the magnetic unit at the rear of the mine, and as he lifted it out there was a fearful explosion. A booby trap charge of between ten and twenty pounds of explosive had gone off. Five men in the shed were killed and others were seriously wounded. Glennie was fortunate enough to escape with his life but was injured in this diabolical attempt to kill off our experts.

In August, 1940, a second attempt was rather crudely made to wipe out our recovery teams. Two mines were dropped, one at the village of Boarhunt, near Portsmouth, the second at Piddlehinton, near Portland. Neither place had the slightest military significance. If the mines had come down at night, this apparently random dropping might have been explained by the faulty navigation of the air crew responsible; but they were dropped in a daylight raid, and the circumstances made it plain that there was nothing random about the targets. These had been chosen carefully in order to bring disposal teams from H.M.S. *Vernon* and from Portland.

The reason was that both mines were elaborately booby trapped; and the intention was that those who tackled them should be killed so spectacularly in the attempt that in the future there would be less enthusiasm in the Royal Navy for recovering unexploded mines. Apart from the suspicion roused by the clumsiness of the attempt, the Boarhunt mine had been partially broken when it fell, and its secrets were easily discovered. The Piddlehinton mine, which occupied the attention of an expert team of R.M.S.O.s for five days, was accidentally blown up during the final stages of stripping. In neither case were there any casualties. The attempt had failed, but it had shown what the Germans were planning to achieve. The logical outcome was a mine which they believed would defy all efforts at recovery.

We therefore laid plans to recover at the first possible opportunity the *EM 1000*.

Orders went out from the Admiralty for a vigilant watch to be kept on all ports, and all R.M.S.O.s and Bomb Disposal Units were told that after an air raid on any area they were to scrutinise most carefully any unexploded bomb or mine. Sooner or later, we believed, one of the new weapons would fall on land and fail to explode.

The first major air attack after we had taken these steps was a blitz on Belfast on April 15th. The city was subjected to a seven-hour concentrated bombardment by up to a hundred aircraft. A number of parachute mines were reported to have dropped, and the Admiralty sent over a Rendering Mines Safe team under Lieutenant-Commander G.G. Turner, R.N.V.R. Turner, who afterwards won the George Cross, had been thoroughly briefed about the expected new weapon. During the two days in which he and his team worked unceasingly helping the overburdened civil defence authorities of Belfast, nothing new was reported to me, and so I flew over to see if I could discover anything.

On my arrival I went to investigate reports of mines falling around a reservoir. In the darkness the raiders had obviously mistaken the glint of the waters of the reservoir for the city's docks. It seemed a likely place to find a *EM 1000*. However, all the mines which had fallen in that area in the hills above the city seemed to have been of the conventional parachute type. There was a report that one of the mines had fallen into the reservoir itself. If this was so, it did not look as if it would be particularly dangerous. There were no ships to set it off, and the hooks of local fishermen would not be sufficiently magnetic to draw a catch like that. The one certain way of finding out if there was anything there was to drain the reservoir, but with the demand for water to fight fires I could not get the local authorities to agree to this. And then, from further inquiries, I decided the whole thing was a false alarm. I reported that there was no mine in the reservoir. It was not until after the war, when we were going through our records, that we decided I might have been a little hasty in this conclusion. We went back and drained the reservoir. Right in the middle, still in deadly working order, was a big parachute mine.

Belfast's ordeal brought no trace of the BM 1000. We returned to London to await the next blitz, wherever it might come.

At the end of the month Merseyside was chosen for attack by the Luftwaffe. Once more we sent off our special investigators, and I waited in London ready to hurry northwards if they discovered what we were seeking.

It was during the raid on Liverpool that one of the most astonishing mine incidents of the war occurred. A parachute mine dropped right on to a gasometer. It drove a hole through the metal top, but instead of crashing on to explode at the bottom it remained suspended by the lines from the parachute, the material of which had caught and held on the outside of the gasometer.

George Newgass, of the Admiralty Land Incident Section, was the officer who had the task of dealing with the situation. Newgass was in his late thirties and came from the West Country, where he had been leading the life of a country squire and was an M.F.H. He wore a monocle and gave the impression of being somewhat languid, regarding mines as a rather tiresome nuisance which had to be cleared away but really were a bit of a bore. It was fortunate that he was so coolly self-possessed. He needed to be.

The pressure in the gasometer had to be maintained in order to prevent the structure from collapsing and so bringing down the mine. Therefore the only practicable approach was through the hole in the top and down into the gas to the mine hanging twenty feet or so below.

If at any moment the parachute cords chafed through and the mine dropped down into the gasometer, or if, possibly by vibration, the fuse was set working, the consequences of an explosion inside the well-filled gasometer would be frightful. The nature of the neighbouring premises added still further to the frightfulness: on one side was a dye works, on the other a munitions factory.

Newgass sent for a diving suit, the only equipment in which he could have air pumped down to him for a sufficient length of time to enable him to do the job. Wearing the diving suit, he was lowered down into the darkness of the gasometer. He reached the mine and went to work to remove the fuse. If it had started to buzz, he would have known nothing about it, because inside the diving helmet he would have been unable to hear. But even if he could have heard, it would have made no practical difference; at the most he would have had twenty seconds in which to be hauled up to the top of the gasometer, descend to the ground and get sufficiently far away to avoid the combined explosions of mine, gasometer, dye works and munitions factory. It was a situation that could ordinarily only be conceived in a nightmare.

Newgass not only survived but lived to receive a well-earned George Medal.

When our investigators completed their search on Merseyside, they still had found no trace of the BM 1000.

At the beginning of May a heavy air attack was launched on Clydeside, which had already been the target of two major raids on successive moonlit nights in March. This time I decided to accompany our special team of R.M.S.O.s to Scotland.

We arrived in Glasgow to find that the area of fresh devastation extended from the city down both banks of the Clyde as far as Greenock. Many parachute mines had been dropped.

I made a quick survey of the area and then settled down to a long, thorough search.

Right: The first BM 1000 photographed as it was found near Dumbarton – it was nearly mistaken for an ordinary bomb.

Below: A complete BM 1000 at Indian Head, Maryland, USA. From left to right are: An un-named scientific officer; Lieutenant Amesbury, USN; Commander Ashe Lincoln; and Commander Darrah, USN, CO of the Magazine Area, Indian Head.

Above: German personnel loading a BM 1000 onto a lorry.

Below: The Dumbarton BM 1000 after it had been dug out. The Sapper officer is six-feet tall

Above: A German mine which has been swept. The plate on the top was to catch fast shallow-draft craft such as MTBs – from it trailed a fifty-foot length of copper wire buoyed at the end with a copper sphere; the slightest contact on the plate or wire was enough to detonate the mine.

Below: An early magnetic mine complete with parachute. The detachable cap on the right acted as a drogue to pull the main parachute canopy from its container.

Above: HMS *Graph* – the former German U-boat *U-570*. The removal of the unused torpedoes from her damaged tubes gave the author some anxiety.

Below: Recovering a German 30-knot torpedo caught by its nose in a torpedo net.

Right: Lieutenant Mould, GC, GM, later promoted Lieutenant-Commander, with a BM 1000.

Below: Lieutenant Tewson, GM, working on the first T-type moored magnetic mine.

Above: Taking in an anti-torpedo net in the Seine Bay.

Below: The Remagen Bridge, which was the first one across the Rhine to be captured intact. The author was responsible for its protection from frogmen attacks.

Above: The nets strung across the Suez Canal.

Below: T-mine tackled by Lieutenant Mould and the author: the poles are to support a rudimentary X-ray apparatus. The mine was hauled ashore by a party safely up on the cliff top.

Left: The author photographed on Malta during his service with the Commandos.

Below: The author sat at his desk.

In Greenock, which had suffered very badly, there were unexploded parachute mines lodged in buildings which had been set ablaze by incendiary bombs. Our R.M.S.O.s had to work fast to disarm these mines and drag them out before flames reached them. We all joined forces to deal with the vast quantities of unexploded incendiary bombs which were lying about.

Near Puddle Deep Beacon, above Port Glasgow, I discovered two mines stuck in sandbanks in the Clyde. Their tails were clearly visible at low water. As the tide receded I was able to wade out to examine them. But they were of the usual parachute type. We could not have rendered them safe between tides, and it would have been foolhardy to try, so I left them to be destroyed by our R.M.S.O.s who would detonate a small charge alongside them.

It took five days of hard work by the Army Bomb Disposal Units and the R.M.S.O.s to complete the routine tasks of clearing up. All unexploded bombs had been found and dealt with, or were awaiting disposal; all but a few of the unexploded mines had been destroyed or made safe. And still there was no trace of the BM 1000. Either it had not been used as a bomb against land targets or it worked with such efficiency that in three major raids not a solitary example had failed to explode. Whatever the explanation we should still have to go on seeking.

To mark the city's gratitude, the Lord Provost of Glasgow gave a civic banquet for all who had helped in the bomb and mine disposal work. This was wholly unexpected, for the city authorities still had more than enough to occupy themselves with in the aftermath of the raid, but it was a very kindly gesture which we very much appreciated. I went along expecting no more than a pleasant evening's relaxation. But it did not turn out like that at all.

We were waiting to go in to dinner, but not too impatiently. Waiters were bringing round trays of drinks; there was the usual chatter and laughter of such occasions; it was a night out, a break in the routine of duty, and we were all ready to enjoy ourselves. After the strain of the past five days, everyone was relieved that the job, as far as he was concerned, was finished. I had not got my BM 1000, but that was no one's fault. It was quite possible that the Germans had not used the new weapon on Clydeside at all. At any rate, we had something to celebrate: we had not suffered a single casualty, and in mine and bomb disposal that was always something for which to be grateful.

A Sapper major sought me out and introduced himself. His name was Bramby, and he commanded the Royal Engineers Bomb Disposal unit. As I was a lieutenant-commander and the senior naval officer present, we were opposite numbers. Bramby and I exchanged the customary pleasantries, and then, suddenly, he said:

"Would you like to see a really good blow-up?"

"Why, what have you got on?"

"Tomorrow morning I'm going to blow up a 'Hermann' I've got down at Dumbarton."

"That's a thousand-kilogramme bomb, isn't it?" I said.

"Yes," said Bramby.

At once a thought crossed my mind, almost too fanciful to be taken seriously. "Are you sure it's a 'Hermann'?"

"Absolutely."

"Have you had to deal with any 'Hermanns' before?"

"Not since my training-school days. Why?"

"Before you blow it up d'you mind if I have a look to make sure it is a 'Hermann'?"

Bramby seemed very slightly taken aback, but he said good-naturedly: "Not at all. Go ahead, old chap."

Sub-Lieutenant Mills, one of the R.M.S.O. party, who was standing in the group where Bramby and I were talking, said: "I've seen the Dumbarton bomb. There's something else down there, too – a broken or partly detonated bomb, and near it are what look like batteries of a wireless set or an acoustic unit."

"Had it a parachute?"

"No," said Mills.

That decided me that there was no time to lose. This might turn out to be a "Hermann" after all, but the fact that there appeared to be wireless or acoustic equipment rather more elaborate than was usual in a bomb seemed promising, and so also was the fact that the two weapons had come down close together.

I said to Mills: "If you don't mind missing your dinner, I'd like you to come down to Dumbarton with me. I want to see that bomb to-night."

"Of course, sir," said Mills, who was an enthusiastic youngster of eighteen or nineteen.

We sent in our apologies to the Lord Provost for absenting ourselves and hurried out to where the car which had been put at my disposal was waiting. I glanced at my watch: it was six-thirty p.m.

"We want to get down to Dumbarton as fast as we can," I said to the Army driver.

"Right, sir. Leave it to me."

The car was a big Humber, red-painted at the front and fitted with a warning bell usual in vehicles employed on mine or bomb disposal work. Even in busy traffic the sight and sound of these vehicles ensured the same clear passage granted to an ambulance or fire engine. We drove smoothly from the city centre and headed down the north bank of the Clyde towards Dumbarton. The reason I was so anxious to get there with the least possible delay was to make sure of enough daylight to try to decide what really had dropped.

On the journey down river I recalled with amusement that it was May 7th. Seven, my father always said, was a lucky number. I am not superstitious, and, as far as I was aware, seven – or for that matter any other number – had never played any "lucky" part in my life. In spite of myself, though, my father's firm belief in the mystic powers of the number seven had always rather impressed me. Now seemed to be an occasion when the theory could be put to the test.

We covered the fifteen miles from Glasgow to Dumbarton in excellent time, and then followed Bramby's directions to reach his "Hermann". We left the town and climbed quite a steep hill on a road running through ploughed farmland.

All along the hills that followed the north bank of the Clyde the R.A.F. had installed a balloon barrage to protect the industrial targets on the riverside from air attack. We stopped the car near one of the balloon sites and started off across the field. Below us, rising massively out of the river, was Dumbarton Rock with its ancient castle. We trod softly to cause the least possible vibration as we approached the shallow crater the weapon had dug in the recently ploughed earth. We had only to go about a hundred yards before we came to Bramby's "Hermann".

The weapon itself was over six feet long – the precise dimensions were later found to be: length, six feet four inches; maximum diameter, twenty-six inches; weight, just under a ton – and from what we could see of it under its partial covering of soil it was pale blue in colour. As this was the usual colour of the big enemy bombs such as the "Hermann" and the "Satan", it was not, at first sight, very encouraging from my point of view. However, Mills and I began to dig away the earth round it with our hands, because it might be unsafe to use tools.

We cleared enough of the soil from the bulbous nose, which had completely buried itself in the earth, to uncover German wording stencilled on to the bomb in vermilion Gothic script: "Zu Verbrauchen bis Marz 1942." All this told us was that, whatever the weapon might be, it was to be used until March, 1942 – that is, it had a further ten months of life. Cautiously, in order that we should not reduce this expectation, and with it our own, we removed more earth from higher up the pale-blue cylindrical shape. We uncovered the lifting lug, which had a black ring painted round it, and a foot or so higher up we came to the fuse which stuck out, nipple-like, an inch or two from the casing. It was a Rheinmetall fuse, and as soon as I saw it my heart sank. This was the standard type of electrical fuse used by the enemy in their bombs; it had never previously been used in mines, which were invariably fitted with clockwork fuses.

Yet, if this was a bomb, it was not an entirely conventional one. All those I had previously seen had been fitted with stout metal fins which were welded into the tail. There was no tail fin to this one; the tail ended in a slightly tapering dome. At the same time, something appeared to have broken off the tail section on impact. Fragments of pale-blue plastic were scattered about the field and these might have formed tail fins; but, if so, they were not the sort usual on bombs.

I was staring at the thing, trying to make up my mind what it was, when a voice said: "Quite a whopper, isn't it, sir?"

Several R.A.F. men from the nearby balloon site had come along to see what was happening to what, no doubt, they regarded as their bomb. They gathered round, highly interested and probably hoping for a bit of excitement.

"It's a proper monster," said one of them. "You know that another of them fell just up the road, sir?"

So completely engrossed had I become with the examination that, momentarily, I had completely forgotten what Mills had said about the second "bomb".

"I'd better go and have a look."

"I'll show you where it is," said the first R.A.F. man, and we all set off together. We had only to go about four hundred yards until we came to a crater where the second "bomb" had detonated and blown up. Mills and I searched the crater and the ground around. As he had said, there were small pieces of mechanism which resembled parts of a wireless set.

"Why on earth should there be a wireless set of this kind inside a bomb?" I wondered. It did not make sense, for it did not seem necessary. But until we knew the purpose of the mechanism, it was not conclusive proof in itself; there had to be further evidence before I could be sure, even in my own mind, that this was not merely a variation of the standard "Hermann".

And then, turning over the soil with my hands, I came upon some greenish material. The light was now beginning to fail, but as the material lay against the palm of my hand there was no doubting its distinctive colour: it was hexanite, an explosive readily distinguishable from the dirty brown, clay-like T.N.T. It also had a different purpose, for while T.N.T. was generally used in aerial bombs, hexanite was used in mines.

The last doubt had disappeared; the picture was now complete and, furthermore, wholly credible. A German minelaying aircraft had flown in from the north, possibly following the valley of the River Leven down from Loch Lomond to Dumbarton. The pilot had dropped down to lay his mines in the Clyde, but not knowing the topography of the area, and possibly distracted by the balloon barrage, he had misjudged his aim and dropped his load short of the river. Half-a-mile farther on and he would have been over the water. Instead, the first of his mines had detonated in a ploughed field and, four hundred yards farther on, just short of the point where the ground plunged steeply down towards the river, the second mine lay almost intact.

Belief, however, is not proof. Although I believed the object that had dug itself into the ploughed furrows of a hillside by the Clyde had brought me to the end of my search for the BM 1000, I could not yet prove this to be so. The evidence was still insufficient to justify my putting through a telephone call to Captain Maitland-Dougall at the Admiralty to say that the BM 1000 had been found. At present, it was still a bomb.

Mills and I continued grubbing away in the crater for all the parts of the second "bomb" we could recover. The more of these we collected and put into a sack which the R.A.F. men let us have, the more convinced I was that they were much too intricate to be part of an ordinary bomb. Finally, when darkness made further search pointless, we took our half-filled sack of bits and pieces back to the car.

We left the R.A.F. men to guard the "bomb" and drove back to Glasgow. The first thing that must be done was to prevent the Army from going ahead with their decision to have "a really good blow-up" next morning. As soon as I got back to the North British Hotel, where I was staying, I put through a telephone call to Major Bramby, and on behalf of the Navy claimed his "Hermann".

"I believe it's a new type of mine," I said. "I'm going to try to render it safe in the morning."

"Good luck, old chap," said Bramby, cordially. "You're welcome to it."

He added that at Army Bomb Disposal Headquarters they already had some large fragments of the detonated "bomb" which we could have. I thanked him and arranged to call round the following morning to pick up these pieces.

Next I put through a call to Naval Headquarters at St. Enoch's Hotel, asking that as soon as Lieutenant Herbert Wadsley, R.N.V.R., reported there in the morning I wanted him to get in touch with me.

Wadsley was an expert R.M.S.O. from H.M.S. *Vernon*, and he was travelling up overnight to Glasgow to dispose of the two magnetic mines which I had found near Puddle Deep Beacon in the bed of the Clyde.

When we met next morning at Naval Headquarters, I told him something much more urgent than the disposal of the two mines had arisen, and I wanted his help.

"It looks as if we've found a BM 1000 at last," I said.

Wadsley was a short, dark man, wiry and very alert mentally. But at the mention of the BM 1000 he looked rather puzzled. I realised then that he had not even heard of the weapon; it was so new that only a limited number of us – those directly involved since the Luftwaffe pilot had boasted that the Germans had a weapon that would defeat Britain within a few weeks – were in on the secret.

I told Wadsley of the information we had so far gleaned about the bomb-mine and the reasons for believing that this was what had dropped at Dumbarton. The one fact I kept from him was that the Germans considered no one would ever render safe the BM 1000 and that, in consequence, special hazards were involved. There seemed nothing to be gained by telling him this. Whether he knew or not, he would still go ahead with the job, although, naturally, if it were made to seem hopeless from the start, his peace of mind must be affected. The point was that the thing had to be tackled, and if he and I did not successfully complete it now, it would fall to someone else later when the next specimen was recovered; there was too much at stake for the job not to be done.

At the same time, Wadsley had to be put on his guard.

"We shall treat this as an ordinary job," I said, "but we shall have to be careful. We do know there is a booby trap in it."

He accepted this information in his usual unruffled way. By nature he was rather quiet and unassuming, and I do not suppose he enjoyed risking his life more than anyone else, but he had prepared himself as well as any man could by making himself thoroughly efficient at the work; and his very considerable experience had given him a calm confidence. For his service on enemy underwater weapons he was later to win the Distinguished Service Cross and the George Medal and Bar.

Before we left Naval Headquarters, there were two matters to arrange: first, to get a signal sent through to Maitland-Dougall at the Admiralty to let him know what we thought we had found and what we were proposing to do about it: and, secondly, to borrow the services of an official photographer from the Flag Officer-in-charge at Glasgow.

We called in at the Army Bomb Disposal Headquarters to see the large fragments of the detonated "bomb" which Bramby had offered. Wadsley examined these and also the "wireless parts" Mills and I had collected from the crater.

"They look like mine mechanism," he said, "but not of any type I've come across before."

When we had completed our examination, the bomb fragments were crated and despatched to the Superintendent of Mine Design in the *Vernon*.

I saw the Army C.O. and asked him if we could have one of his bomb experts to assist us with the Rheinmetall fuse. This was something that neither Wadsley nor I had experience in handling. A tall, powerfully-built Sapper, Lieutenant Gerald, at once volunteered to go with us. Our party was completed by Lieutenant Fenwick, G.M., R.N.V.R., one of our own R.M.S.O.s,

Chief Petty Officer Salter and Able Seaman Mountford. We set off for Dumbarton.

At the site of the detonated "bomb" we gathered together quantities of the green material I had identified as hexanite and set it on fire, as this was one of the tests for hexanite. It burned with all the brilliance of sparklers at a children's bonfire-night party. There was no doubt that it was hexanite, which is something like forty per cent aluminium.

The next thing was to scrape away with our hands as much earth as possible from the "bomb" that had fallen more or less intact so that the photographer could get pictures from as many angles as possible. He was then sent back to Glasgow to process his pictures at once and rush them off by special messenger to Maitland-Dougall at DTMI. Even if the "bomb" blew up during our attempts to make it safe, there would at least be an adequate record of its appearance.

There was one other precaution to be taken in case of accidents. This was for Fenwick to stay some distance from the "bomb" itself while we worked on it, observing us as we carried out each planned operation so that if anything went wrong he would know exactly at what stage we had met trouble.

Sergeant Macleod and Constable Thomson of the Dumbarton Burgh Police joined us to see if they could be of any help. I accepted their offer as their presence would ensure that we should not be troubled by sightseers or by traffic on the road which might result in dangerous vibration.

Every possible eventuality now seemed to have been covered, so we went to work. The time was twelve noon.

On these jobs, the preparation and anticipation were always the worst part. It was then that natural apprehension was at its greatest. Once the task began, it was never so bad.

Gerald had a stethoscope which he lent to Wadsley. Wadsley sounded the blue cylindrical shape all over its exposed surface.

"I can hear no ticking," he said.

This, at any rate, was a relief. It meant that either it was not operated by clockwork, or, if it was, that the clockwork had stopped. If he had heard ticking, we should have had no means of knowing at what moment it might blow up.

Gerald examined the fuse.

"Rheinmetall," he said, "but of an unusual kind. The number is unusual also – 157/3. The highest number so far has been in the region of the fifties."

The sudden jump in the serial number suggested that the fuse was specially designed for a particular purpose. The evidence was steadily building up to proof that this was in fact a BM 1000.

Gerald unscrewed the cap of the fuse.

"The fuse itself appears to be quite loose," he said.

We knew that frequently the Germans fitted a booby trap behind the fuse. The booby trap was operated by a spring when the fuse was lifted from its socket.

Wadsley and I squatted beside the "bomb" to test the fuse for a booby trap. While he unscrewed the keep ring which held it in place, I pressed two fingers down on the fuse to prevent it from springing out of its socket should it be booby trapped. When the keep ring was finally removed, I eased my pressure on the fuse very slightly.

"It seems firm," I said. "You try it."

Wadsley put his hand on the fuse as I took my fingers away.

"I think," he said, "I can feel it lifting."

If he was right, there was only one thing to do: that was to run. Together we hared across the field. Under the compulsion of what might at any moment happen behind us, we covered two hundred yards in considerably better than average time. We flung ourselves flat on the soft earth, breathless, ears pounding from the exertion. With painful slowness, it seemed, the second hand on the watch on my outstretched wrist ticked off a minute. And nothing happened. The second minute passed. Still nothing happened.

Wadsley and I got up and returned to the crater. We crouched down and placed our ears to the fuse. But no sound came from it.

"It might be safer to remove the fuse from a distance."

"I think so, too."

Wadsley fetched a long length of line and with great care secured one end round the top of the fuse. We retired to a distance of about three hundred yards and lay down. Wadsley gave the line a sharp pull. At first the fuse resisted, but after several tugs it seemed to come out. We waited for the explosion. We gave it two minutes. But nothing happened.

We returned to the "bomb", as catfooted as our uniform shoes would allow. The fuse was still firmly in place. The line had slipped off with the tugging.

I had a shot at fastening the line. This was not easy since there was so little of the fuse protruding from the casing, but I managed to secure a clove hitch around it, and once more we retired and laid flat.

Again and again we tugged on the line, but once more it came adrift from the fuse.

Gerald said: "You'll never get it out that way. Here, I've got a grip – use that."

Fenwick rigged a shackle and a length of wire to Gerald's special grip. The line was made fast to the wire. Gerald screwed the grip to the fuse, and for the third time we retired, lay down and tugged.

This time the fuse came out. We waited a full minute but there was no explosion, and we went back to see what had happened.

The fuse hung loosely from three wires running into the interior of the casing. Two of the wires were red, the third was black. The red wires led towards the tail of the bomb.

At the base of the fuse socket there was a small detonator cap and a gaine, around which were placed the usual picric rings of the primer. Together they formed an explosive chain: the detonator contained highly sensitive fulminate of mercury, and this set off the less sensitive picric of the primer, which in turn set off the gaine, a length of explosive tape leading to the main charge. Inserting his fingers into the fuse hole, Wadsley began to pull out the picric rings. When he reached the last one, he spotted something red beneath it.

"It looks like another detonator," he said.

I had a look down the fuse hole, and agreed with him. We decided it might be highly dangerous to probe further, so the last picric ring was left in position.

We next went to work on the after part of the "bomb", which had slightly broken away from the main body. The fracture was little more than a crack where the tail cone joined the main shell containing the explosive charge. It was in this tail section, we surmised, that the mine mechanism must be installed, if in fact this was a mine.

We had now come to the most critical point of the operation.

If this was a mine and the Germans followed their usual practice, it was here that we should find the booby trap. All previous booby traps in enemy mines had worked by means of a spring-loaded plunger set against the rear part of the weapon. When the after part was removed to reach the mechanism, the plunger was released and the booby trap exploded.

Ordinarily, the presence of a booby trap could be spotted by a small examination plughole on the outside of the casing. But we could find no such hole. This meant the booby trap, if there was one, must be of a kind we had not come up against before.

Whatever we did now, we were dealing with the unknown. There was no book on this one. We were strictly on our own, and we had to find the answers ourselves.

We tried to visualise what lay behind the pale-blue casing.

"There must be electric wires leading to any booby trap."

"The only thing to do is to bore holes in the casing to see if we can locate them."

Wadsley fetched his brace and bit. He began to bore through the metal shell. It was quite soft, and the bit went through readily.

He shone his torch into the hole and peered inside.

He bored more holes close to the junction of the main body and the tapering tail section. But as he squinted into each tiny peep-hole in turn he saw nothing in the beam of his torch which enabled us to decide where the booby trap was or how it might operate.

The crack in the casing between the main part of the "bomb" and the tail looked as if it had completely severed one section from the other. The tail unit seemed loose enough to come away, but we decided not to attempt to separate it in case that set off the booby trap. Wadsley shone his torch through the narrow aperture to see what he could discern in the tail compartment.

"It looks as if it's filled with batteries," he said.

The time was three p.m. We had been working on the "bomb" for three hours.

The only course now was for us to dig the bomb out of the crater. For this we should need help. We drove down to Dumbarton to see the local Army commander, who at once agreed to supply equipment and a digging party.

I telephoned to Maitland-Dougall at the Admiralty to let him know how things were going, and he said: "I've arranged for an X-ray apparatus to be sent up to examine the object for booby traps before you go any further."

But the X-ray apparatus had to come up from Nottingham, and, as the transport bringing it had left only in the last quarter-of-an-hour, it was unlikely to reach Dumbarton before the following afternoon.

We went back to the crater and set about digging to clear a good space all round the "bomb" ready for the X-ray apparatus to be used. Everyone turned to with spades, the Army C.O., the two policemen, all of us. At five o'clock three soldiers arrived to lend a hand.

Eventually, all was ready for the X-ray examination, and it was then that I had to leave the site. That evening I had to return to London by the night train to deliver at the Admiralty a detailed report on the progress that had been made. I left Wadsley in charge.

Next day, when the X-ray gave no indication of a booby trap, he separated the two sections of the "bomb" at the break in the casing and severed the wires which were found to link them. It was now safe to load the weapon on to a lorry to take it to H.M.S. *Vernon* for dissection and detailed examination.

By then we knew there was no doubt as to the true identity of Bramby's "Hermann": stencilled on the under side of the charge case was the marking BM 1000.

As soon as the BM 1000 reached *Vernon*, I went down there to join Wadsley in the task of stripping it down. This was a precaution adopted since the fatalities caused by the explosion of the booby trap in Glennie's mine, so that the scientists who conducted the final exhaustive dissection should not unnecessarily be exposed to danger. When the scientists arrived in the mining shed to carry out the post mortem examination, I stayed on to give them what help I could. Besides, I was most anxious to learn what they would discover about the workings of BM 1000.

In calling the weapon a *Bombemine*, the Germans had precisely described its function.

If it fell on hard ground, it was designed to go off like a bomb, exploding instantly by the action of an inertia pellet switch in the Rheinmetall bomb-type fuse. If it fell on any other surface, the fuse would operate the switch in the mine unit, arming the weapon and making it capable of functioning in a number of ways. On soft ground, in mud or in water less than twenty-four feet deep, a delay device completed the main detonator circuit after an interval of ninety seconds to two minutes and exploded the mine. Finally, if the mine was laid in water deeper than twenty-four feet and the water level subsequently fell below this level, or if the mine was moved into shallower water, a hydrostatic valve would operate to blow it up.

In water over twenty-four feet deep it operated as a magnetic mine. The magnetic unit was housed under the dome of the tail.

As a magnetic mine, the BM 1000 had considerable advantages over any previous airborne type used, since in the laying it did not require a parachute. It was the parachute which often caught the eye of mine-watchers, who were then able to pinpoint the position where mines had been laid. With the new mine there was no such risk of detection.

Despite the elaborate and ingenious multiplicity of methods devised to prevent the BM 1000 from falling into our hands intact, the Germans had nonetheless considered the possibility of all these failing. To prevent us exploiting such a failure, they had included also a rare form of booby trap.

If the dome of the tail containing the mechanism broke off, or was removed as had been done at Dumbarton, two small circular glass windows were exposed. Behind the windows were highly sensitive photo-electric cells. Any light of any colour or intensity greater than twilight reaching either window caused the cells to send a current to a detonator which blew up the whole mine.

When I learned of this, I recalled Wadsley with his brace and bit boring holes in the casing, not only letting in the sunlight but sending his torch beam right into the heart of the mine; and not merely directing the beam into the little peep-holes but keeping it shining for quite a long period into the crack where the tail unit had broken away from the main charge. And as I thought of it, my blood ran cold.

If ever two men could claim to be lucky, then Wadsley and I could. Our experience was in fact unique. Never afterwards was a BM 1000 made safe in daylight; the work was always done in pitch darkness, by touch alone.

We owed our good fortune solely to the fact that the short length of wire which led from the booby trap to the detonator had snapped when the mine hit solid earth. It was possibly a chance in a million. Otherwise we should have been blasted to eternity, and Goering's boast that the mine was irrecoverable would have been believed.

Hour after hour, the scientists continued with their post mortem examination. Midnight came and passed. I had difficulty in keeping my eyes open. After the strain of the past few days, when very little sleep had been possible, I was almost dizzy from fatigue.

The Mines Commander, noticing the state I was in, came over and said: "You can't be of any further use here, Lincoln. You must get some sleep."

It was nearly two a.m., but despite this he telephoned to his wife at their home in the village outside Portsmouth and asked her to make some coffee and get a room ready. Then he drove me out to the house in his car and sent me off to bed with the promise to call for me next day.

By eight o'clock that morning I was back in the *Vernon* unable to rest any longer until I knew what final conclusions the scientists had reached. These were of vital importance. Not only had the *BM 1000* been designed so that it would never fall intact into our hands, its mechanism had been evolved so that we should never be able to sweep it to clear the shipping channels. At least, not by our present methods.

The Double-ell sweep, which had up to now proved so successful, operated an electric pulse lasting five seconds. This was perfectly adequate to detonate any magnetic mines so far laid by the enemy. But, with its five-second pulse, the Double-ell would have passed harmlessly over the *BM 1000*, Channels could have been swept and declared clear for shipping and only when some luckless merchantman went to the bottom would it have been discovered that they were still mined. However, from what the scientists had discovered, we were now in a position to change that. By increasing the duration of the electric pulse the Double-ell could be made as effective against the new danger as it had been against the old. It would require alterations of the equipment to achieve this, but now it was known what changes had to be made the channels could be swept clear.

Not long after my return to the *Vernon* the telephone rang. It was the Admiralty on the line, and the Director of Torpedoes and Mining himself wanted to speak to me.

He wasted no time on preliminaries. "Have you found the answer to the *BM 1000* yet?"

"Yes, sir. The thing works on an eleven-second pulse."

"Thank God for that," he said. "Last night the Germans filled the Suez Canal with them."

Thus, by the narrowest possible margin, we were able to foil the German attempt to cut the supply line to our Forces in the

Middle East at the moment when they were fighting for survival in Greece, Crete and in the Western Desert. The irony, of course, was that our success had come about because two months before, in an outburst of anger, a Luftwaffe pilot had chosen to prophesy Britain's defeat, and so had given us the first clue to the *BM 1000*.

Postscript: Twelve days after the Admiralty had informed our naval commands by top secret letter of the details of the *BM 1000*, now designated German Type-G mine, Hitler attacked Russia. In accordance with the British Government's promise to Stalin to keep our new ally informed about our discoveries of the secrets of Nazi weapons, full details of the Type-G mine, together with drawings, were passed on to the Russians. The Russians were told that the Germans were unaware of our knowledge of this weapon and enjoined to keep the fact a strict secret. To our astonishment and utter dismay the full details of the *BM 1000*, illustrated with pictures, were published for the whole world to see in *Pravda*! Although we have no proof that this was so, we believed that in consequence the Germans may have incorporated new booby traps in the *BM 1000* and that these later led to the death of at least one of our R.M.S.O.s.

Chapter 8

The *U-570*

As a naval investigator one always had to be prepared at a moment's notice to turn one's hand to the most diverse practical problems. Training fitted one to tackle most of these quite satisfactorily, but there were times when a specialist skill was required that had not been included in training. Once, for example, I was almost obliged to become an oxy-acetylene welder, a highly specialised trade for which none of my past training had remotely equipped me. Under the circumstances, it was fortunate that I received a last-minute reprieve, or this account might not now be written.

The reason I came to contemplate the use of a rather fearsome acetylene torch arose, indirectly, from the capture of the German submarine *U-570*, complete with crew. The capture, one of the most strikingly dramatic successes of the war, was a triumph for the Royal Air Force. The story of that exploit, on August 27, 1941, has been fully told, so it is necessary only briefly to recall the facts.

While on patrol eighty miles south of Iceland, a Lockheed Hudson aircraft of Coastal Command spotted the U-boat on the surface. The submarine dived before her commander realised his presence had been observed. The aircraft marked the spot where the submarine had submerged, and when she surfaced a couple of hours later there was another Hudson waiting to deal with her. The time was then about 10.30 a.m. The submarine attempted to reach safety by diving, but the Hudson dropped depth charges which caused sufficient damage to make the Germans think better of chancing escape below the surface. When they made to man their anti-aircraft guns, the Hudson soon put an end to that with machine-gun fire.

The German commander, Hans Rahmlow, now found himself in the position where he could not – or would not – dive; could not – or would not – risk fighting it out with the aircraft. He resolved his dilemma by waving his white shirt in token of surrender. The Hudson, operating in the sort of weather found usually in the area of Iceland, kept the submarine in this state of surrender until relieved by other aircraft. These circled the vessel until well into the night, when a trawler arrived to make sure that the Germans did not try to scuttle their ship or to use the cover of darkness to get away. By this time, according to the official record, the submariners – or, at any rate, the bulk of them – had little thought of getting away; they were seasick and thoroughly demoralised. When morning came, a destroyer and more trawlers arrived. The U-boat crew were taken off, and their ship was towed to Iceland.

The fact that this particular crew, making their first war-time cruise, did not give a very impressive account of themselves should not be taken as being in any way typical of German U-boat seamen. They were a tough, well-disciplined breed and highly skilled in their job. The fact that they were responsible for more than seventy per cent of the thirty thousand casualties suffered by our Merchant Navy proved how formidable a force they were. The attitude of German submariner prisoners towards some of the officers of the *U-570* was far more characteristic of the service than was that of the crew who surrendered.

It is said that Rahmlow only missed facing a "trial" held by a group of senior German U-boat officers at Grizedale Hall, Lake Windermere, by being transferred to another prisoner-of-war camp. Already, his second in command, Bernhard Berndt, who had preceded him to Grizedale Hall, had been called upon to answer for his conduct and had been judged guilty of cowardice.

There are two versions of Berndt's subsequent behaviour.

The first is that his fellow officers were so angered by his conduct that they told him bluntly they found his presence intolerable. Unless he wished to suffer the consequences, he must make his escape from the camp; Grizedale Hall was too small to hold them and him.

The second explanation is that, in order to try to redeem his conduct, he offered to escape and make his way to Barrow-in-Furness to sabotage the *U-570* which had been brought from Iceland and was now in dry dock at Vickers' yard. This would seem to have been a venture doomed from the start, even if he had known where the submarine was.

Whatever the circumstances preceding his leaving the camp, the fact is that he broke out. It is also a fact that he was picked up by Home Guards and, in a further attempt to escape, he was shot and killed.

From the point of view of the German Navy, the loss of the submarine was a singularly ignominious affair. The general view at the time was that the crew of the *U-570*, if they had had the determination, could have got away by diving their vessel; she was still in a condition to submerge, even if there was some risk in doing so. But if it was the buckled state of the forward plating of his vessel which caused the German commander to avoid chancing a crash-dive, then I must confess a certain sympathy for him: those buckled bow plates caused me also to suffer several very uncomfortable hours.

For the Royal Navy, the acquisition of the *U-570* was a magnificent prize. The technical specialists of several branches hurried to Barrow to set about discovering the secrets of the German submarine which could be turned to our advantage in the war against the U-boats. Since the full quota of electric torpedoes were still in their tubes – four forward and one aft – we at DTMI had a major interest in the capture, first to get the torpedoes out of the submarine and make them safe, and secondly to find out all there was to know about their operation. This task was given to one of our officers, Lieutenant Martin Johnson, R.N.R.

On his arrival at Barrow, he inspected the submarine and then telephoned me at the Admiralty.

"This job is much more complicated than we anticipated," he said. "We can't get at the torpedoes. The bow plates are crushed in on the top of the torpedo tubes."

"And they can't be retracted from the tubes?"

"No, the submarine has no machinery working, so that is impossible. It might be dangerous even if it were possible. The torpedoes may be damaged and in a dangerous condition."

I knew that the question of danger did not bother Johnson personally – he subsequently was awarded the George Medal – but he was most anxious that nothing should be done to endanger the submarine; she was much too precious to risk damaging.

"I'll come up to assist you," I said, and set off at once for Barrow. There was no time to be lost, because the longer we took making the torpedoes safe the greater the delay before the other specialists could get to work on the submarine and her equipment. Next morning I arrived at the shipyard.

From the bottom of the dry dock a wooden staging had been erected up to the bows of the *U-570*. With Johnson I climbed up to see the extent of the damage. It was obvious that the torpedoes would never be taken out of the tubes in their present state.

"The only thing we can do," I said, "is to get someone with an oxy-acetylene torch to cut away the crushed steel plates."

The prospect of standing up on the staging while this was done did not appeal to me in the least. The heat from the torch might be sufficient to cause the T.N.T. charge to burn, and that in turn could set off the sensitive explosives in the pistols in the warheads of the torpedoes. If that happened there would be very little left of the *U-570* and nothing at all of ourselves. To make matters worse, it was raining – a dismal, cheerless, wet Sunday morning.

I found a group of shipyard welders and told them what was wanted.

"It is only fair to say," I added, "that there is a certain amount of danger to this job."

"How many torpedoes are there?" said one of the men.

"Four."

"And how much explosive in each torpedo?"

"Five hundred pounds."

The thought of being at close quarters when nearly a ton of explosive might well go off was clearly as distasteful to them as it was to me. They, however, had one advantage: they could perfectly reasonably refuse to have any part of it. This they proceeded to do. I did not blame them. They were mostly middle-aged married men, and it was not in their contract that they had to risk blowing themselves up.

"Of course, I'll be up there with whoever does this job."

This offer of my company did not cause them to regard the prospect of eternity with any greater relish; they declined with the same emphasis as before.

By now I was beginning to feel a little desperate. Having come up to help Johnson, it seemed to me that as his senior I must do something to get the job done.

"All right," I said to the men, "if one of you will show me how to use the oxy-acetylene torch, I'll do it myself."

There was a few moments' silence, and then one of the men, rather younger than the rest, stepped forward and said: "I'll do the job for you."

We climbed back on to the staging, and he fetched up his equipment in readiness.

"Don't worry about this," I said, trying to sound as casual as possible. "I'll show you where to cut. If you cut carefully, all will be well."

The welder tested his torch, adjusting it so that the flame was exactly as he would require it. It burned with an intense and brilliant heat.

The welder, Johnson and I stood up on the staging, all feeling very tense. We forgot the discomfort of the rain; we were too occupied with the task of pretending that this was just a routine job of cutting some steel plating.

I marked with my forefinger the area of metal that had to be removed around the first tube to give access to the torpedo.

Johnson, who was a probation officer in civil life, had not before, I knew, been called on to render safe German torpedoes, although he was fully trained to do so. I had not before tackled a German torpedo, either. It would have been more reassuring if one of us had done so.

"All right," I said to the welder. "Start now."

He brought his torch close to the plating. There was a shower of sparks. The flame bit through the metal. The ease with which it melted away the stout plating only emphasised the amount of heat that was being generated. Clearly, the heat must be conducted through the surrounding plating to the torpedo tube and so to the torpedo.

And, of course, to the T.N.T.

We stared through the fierce rain of sparks as the flame cut into the metal, and we were needlessly taut, for if anything happened it would have been so swift that there would have been nothing we could have done to save ourselves.

The welder worked carefully, keeping precisely to the line I had indicated. At last the first tube was clear of crushed plates. We lifted away the battered metal and laid it on the staging.

I pointed out the area to be cut around the second tube, and the welder set to work on that. By the time the second tube was clear, we were feeling very much better. Two of the torpedoes had been exposed to the heat of the oxy-acetylene torch without anything happening. We were half way to success. Again we became conscious of the fact that it was raining and we were being thoroughly soaked. To be aware of the chill discomfort was a welcome release from the strain of over-stretched nerves.

The work went on. The third tube was cleared. We were now sufficiently optimistic to enjoy the luxury of cursing the rain.

The flame was turned on to the plating surrounding the fourth tube. The sparks showered. The metal parted under the heat. The welder moved his torch with steady assurance, cutting carefully, surely. He was a good, skilful workman. Only four inches to go, three, two … the final inch of crushed plating vanished. The torch was extinguished. The four tubes were clear.

"That was a first-class job," I said, thankfully.

The welder pushed up his protective goggles. His face was pallid and streaked with grime, but he had lost the look of strain.

"Always try to help the Navy, sir," he grinned.

Now Johnson and I could get down to the job of rendering safe the torpedoes. First, we had to remove the pistols.

The torpedo pistol was rather like a miniature torpedo itself. It protruded several inches from the nose of the torpedo and extended well back into the warhead. It was fitted with a small propeller which was rotated by the thrust of the torpedo through the water; this propeller armed the pistol by bringing the detonators into such a position that they could be struck by the strikers. Around the propeller were clustered four metal "whiskers", like double antennae. When these "whiskers" were pressed back by a blow of more than eighty pounds' pressure, they caused the spring-release of the steel strikers. The strikers fired six detonators, which set off two very sensitive primers, and these in turn exploded the five hundred pounds of T.N.T. which packed the warhead.

Removal of each pistol was a simple matter of unscrewing the two holding nuts on the nose of the torpedo and withdrawing the cylindrical shape from its cavity in the warhead. We carried the pistols down off the staging on to the dockside.

The important thing was that the *U-570* was now safe for the experts to go aboard to collect all the information they wanted, and when they had finished gathering the German secrets the submarine was ready to be repaired and refitted to go to sea as H.M.S. *Graph*. Under this name and manned by the Royal Navy she not only lived down her sorry start but won distinction worthy of the skill that had gone into her design and construction.

The pistol which had been taken from the torpedo in the submarine's stern by a *Vernon* specialist officer was added to our four from the bow tubes. Johnson and I made off with these to the remotest corner of the yard we could find. Rendering these safe might prove the most dangerous part of our day's work.

We assumed that the German pistols would have detonators and primers installed separately as in our own, but we had no means of knowing just where along the length of the pistol these two lots of explosive might be situated. The forward end of the pistol was made of phosphor-bronze, which was very hard, but the after part was of soft aluminium. We decided to saw through that to see what was inside.

Using a hacksaw, we cut through the soft metal with some caution. Since the hacksaw blade was straight and the pistol case was cylindrical, there must have come a moment in the cutting when the blade was at some depth inside the concave underside of the casing. It was at those moments that we had most cause to sweat. The friction of the blade cutting into the detonators or primers might easily have produced sufficient heat to touch them off.

As we worked, a highly-decorated submarine commander came over to see what we were doing. He left us to it, with the not too comforting remark: "I'd rather you were doing that than me!"

We continued sawing until we had cut through the first of the pistols. Next came the task of removing the detonators and primers. Here we discovered that the explosive content of the German pistols was differently arranged from our own. Instead of being separate, they were married; the detonators were set into the primers, which meant a bigger explosion if a detonator fired during the rendering safe. To move the detonators we had to use a screwdriver, and to get a grip with it we had to exert a fair amount of pressure. The worrying part was that as we pushed home the screwdriver it was liable to slip, and if it slipped it might blow up the detonator – and, with it, the primer. This in fact proved the trickiest part of the whole operation.

But now that we knew the position of the detonators and primers, we were able to make safe the remaining four pistols by unscrewing on each the keep ring between the nose and the aluminium part.

Eventually, the work was done.

It had been the longest, wettest Sunday in my recollection.

A fortnight after I returned to London from Barrow, a signal reached the Admiralty to say that a German torpedo of the type we had removed from the *U-570* had run ashore in Dutch Guiana. The Royal Dutch Navy wanted to render it safe and dissect it, and they would welcome any guidance we could give. In reply, we signalled off detailed instructions telling them precisely how we had gone about the task. What happened exactly we do not know – perhaps we had been enormously lucky; but when the Dutchmen came to render safe the pistol it unfortunately blew up and seven of them were killed.

Chapter 9

To Sea with the Champion Minesweeper

While my work at the Admiralty was utterly absorbing and offered frequent opportunities to travel – indeed, by the time the war ended my duty journeys amounted to many thousands of miles – it was travel almost entirely by land or air. The occasions when I even set foot on a ship's deck were extremely few. And since all my life I have been at heart a seaman, and for this reason had determined to serve in the Royal Navy, the rare chances to go to sea, however short the passage, were always welcome. My one regret is that they occurred so infrequently. One of the occasions at sea that I particularly recall was in November, 1941.

The circumstances which led to it arose from the fact that the Flag Officer in charge of the Humber area and the commanders of his minesweepers found themselves confronted with this problem: after the approach channels to the estuary had been thoroughly swept and declared safe for shipping, underwater explosions were still occurring, some of them dangerously close to minesweepers, *even though no fresh mines had been laid*.

Guy Postlethwaite, a lieutenant of the R.N.V.R. and one of our mine experts in DTMI, was sent up to Grimsby to try to solve the mystery. His orders were to go out with the Humber minesweepers to investigate the incidents at first hand. It was arranged that he should join the *Rolls Royce*, a minesweeping trawler under the command of Skipper Leopold Romyn,

R.N.R., who was a Unit Commander and had charge of a group of minesweepers.

By the time Postlethwaite reached the base, the trawlers had left harbour, so he had to embark at sea. There was half a gale blowing when the tender which took him out from Grimsby went alongside the *Rolls Royce*. Both the tender and minesweeper were pitching and rolling wildly in the heavy seas. Postlethwaite managed to sling his gear aboard the minesweeper, but when he jumped the gap between the two vessels his foot slipped and he was left hanging by his hands from the gunwale of the *Rolls Royce*. Before the crew could haul him inboard, tender and minesweeper surged together. Postlethwaite was swept from his handhold and dropped into the sea, crushed between the steel plates of the two vessels. The trawlermen rescued him alive but severely injured. He was put ashore and rushed to Grimsby hospital.

As soon as we at the Admiralty received news of the accident, I was ordered to go to Grimsby to take over the investigation. On my arrival, I went to see Postlethwaite in hospital. By great good fortune, his spine had not been broken by the crushing he had received, nor was he likely to suffer permanent disablement; but he would be out of action for a long time. However, he was able to pass on to me such information as he had been able to glean from officers at the base and I left him to join the *Rolls Royce*.

The vessel was still out on minesweeping operations, so I put off by tender. There was still a heavy sea running, and transferring was a tricky business. But I was luckier than Postlethwaite and managed to transfer from ship to heaving ship in safety.

The name may perhaps give rather a grander picture than the reality: for *Rolls Royce* was a converted fishing trawler, thirty years old and typical of the sturdy, workaday ships which keep to the sea under the most abominable conditions, even during the Arctic winter, to bring back their catches to Grimsby. She was tough and salty, and so, too, was Skipper Romyn, her commanding officer.

He was a legendary character in the fishing industry, and an action of his while awaiting the result of his application to join the Navy as a Patrol Service skipper shows the nature of the man. Two German mines broke loose from their moorings and were swept towards the shore at Yarmouth. If they had gone off, they might well have caused immense damage to the town. Romyn removed this threat by plunging into a raging sea and roping the mines securely. He and his fellow skippers in the Humber area, along with their Royal Naval Patrol Service crews, carried one of the heaviest burdens of the war; of all the East Coast waters, the Humber was probably the most consistently mined by the Germans. The locally based minesweepers, mostly converted fishing trawlers, notched up some of the top minesweeping records by the time the war ended.

As soon as my gear was heaved aboard the *Rolls Royce*, we went off to start minesweeping.

All the trawlers in the Humber force were fitted with the Double-ell sweep. To work the sweep, they steamed in pairs abreast. Astern of the leading pair, the others took up station in echelon. A dan-laying trawler usually brought up the rear to mark with her buoys the extent of the cleared channel.

Each minesweeper towed a pair of buoyant cables, or tails, with an electrode at the end; the outer cable was 750 yards long, the inner one, towed from the side of the vessel facing her sister ship, was 175 yards in length. At six-second intervals both trawlers emitted a pulse of electric current through the cables. This created a magnetic field between the two long tails strong enough to detonate any enemy magnetic mine lying on the sea-bed within the rectangle formed. The current passing through the short tails neutralised this magnetic field in the immediate vicinity of the trawler herself, so that in theory no enemy magnetic mine could explode close to a minesweeper.

Shortly after we started sweeping, that theory was exploded quite literally. The stern of the *Rolls Royce* was jerked upwards as though by a giant hand, and several tons of water were flung into the air and then deluged down on to the ship. We were hurled off our feet by the force of the explosion. As we picked ourselves up, half-stunned, a rating rushed up to the bridge shouting: "The ship's on fire!"

This proved, fortunately, to be less alarming than it sounded. What had happened was that the blast of the mine, which had gone off twenty or thirty yards astern, had blown the galley fire clean out of the stove and on to the deck outside. Spray falling on the glowing coals had set up a cloud of steam which made it appear that the ship herself was ablaze.

The fact that the explosion had occurred in a channel which had already been swept and where no fresh mines had been laid was striking proof of the seriousness of the problem. We continued with the sweeping, but it was not long before the second explosion occurred. This one was disastrous.

Our sister minesweeper, steaming along some four hundred yards on our beam, abruptly disappeared in a colossal gout of smoke and flame. Romyn at once headed the *Rolls Royce* towards the spot, but when we arrived there was no trace of the trawler or her crew. It seemed fantastic that the sea could have swallowed both ship and men so utterly and so swiftly, but this was what had happened. A mine must have detonated immediately beneath the trawler, and she had disintegrated completely.

This shocking end to one of his ships and her crew, whom he knew well, must have affected Romyn deeply, but except for the fact that his expression became grimmer he hid his feelings. He ordered the trawler *D.W. Fitzgerald*, one of a pair of minesweepers astern, to move up and partner *Rolls Royce* in the lead. As soon as she was in position, sweeping began again. The disaster we had witnessed was one of the everyday hazards faced by the men of the minesweepers; there could be no let-up in the essential work of clearing the channels.

But mines were not the only hazard with which the crews had to contend. As we were sweeping near to the coast, we heard the wail of air-raid sirens ashore. An enemy hit-and-run raid was about to be staged on some unfortunate seaside town.

Suddenly, from the low clouds above us, a pair of Heinkels dived, making straight for our little group of ships. The minesweeper gunners were at action stations, and at once opened fire with all guns. The Heinkel crews had possibly assumed we were ill-armed merchantmen, and the concentration of fire that met them was more than they had bargained for. They pulled out of their dive and roared back into the cover of the clouds.

Two more aircraft flashed into view, heading towards us. Again a solid mass of anti-aircraft fire rose from the cluster of trawlers. Both aircraft banked abruptly and sheered away from us. It was only as they did so that we saw the R.A.F. roundels on their wings.

"Ah, well," said Romyn, "it doesn't do to take chances."

As the sweep continued, another mine blew up close to the *Rolls Royce*, fortunately without causing damage or casualties. A little later the fourth mine of the day went off, seemingly right in the path of the *D.W. Fitzgerald*.

We waited anxiously for the smoke and spray to clear, fearing that she had shared the fate of her predecessor, but to our relief she steamed into view through the cascading spray, intact.

Painted on her bows was the number 1820, which reminded me of the well-known advertisement for a certain famous brand of whisky. At my suggestion, Romyn sent this congratulatory signal: "Good old *Johnny Walker* – still going strong!"

But there was no response from the *D.W. Fitzgerald*. When we met ashore afterwards, her skipper asked Romyn: "What the hell was the idea of your curious signal? You know damn well my ship isn't the *Johnny Walker*."

Obviously, whisky was not that skipper's favourite tipple, either.

When dusk came, our minesweeping duties were over for the day, but this was when the trawlers switched their role and became convoy escorts up and down the coast. As the stretch of coast they covered had become notorious as "E-boat Alley", escort work was as great a strain and headache as minesweeping.

We were waiting to join our convoy when we heard the heavy drumming of aircraft engines approaching from the land. Bomber Command, from their bases in Yorkshire and Lincolnshire, were mounting a night raid on Germany.

Above the throb of the engines came staccato bursts of machine-gun fire. It was the practice of R.A.F. gunners to test their weapons by firing off a number of rounds into the sea, and this was what we imagined was happening now. But as the aircraft passed overhead we saw to our amazement that the fire from their guns was spattering across the sea towards the trawlers.

"The bastards are shooting at us!" roared a furious voice.

The trawler skippers switched on recognition lights to show that we were friendly vessels and not the enemy which, presumably, the airmen reckoned us to be. But still the sea around us was dancing with the splash of cannon shells. The next thing was that both the *Rolls Royce* and the next astern, *Ben Meidie*, a sister ship, were hit.

"Can't the fools realise what they're doing?"

"Someone's going to be killed if they keep this up."

The trawlermen were excusably angered by what appeared to them to be sheer stupidity on the part of the air crews.

"There's only one way to stop this," said Romyn. "Retaliation."

Our guns opened up on our own aircraft. All at once, realisation dawned on the airmen. They, too, began flashing recognition signals. Luckily, although our fire had been heavy, the engagement ended with no casualties on either side.

By the time we joined our flock of merchantmen and started off southward, the night was dark and there was a heavy sea running. The hours slowly passed. We rolled and wallowed, striving to keep station on the convoy in the thick, wild darkness.

At about 2.30 a.m., off the Norfolk coast, the inevitable pack of E-boats tore into the slow huddle of merchantmen. Gun flashes lit the sky and tracer ripped through the darkness. The encounter was short and fierce, and the E-boats streaked off to seaward again. One merchantman was torpedoed, but she was the only casualty on our side – and she did not sink but was towed safely into port.

Later that morning we transferred the convoy to a new escort and headed off back to the Humber. The wind had been strengthening all night, and soon we were driving almost straight into a north-easterly gale. The trawlers rode the seas splendidly, but we still took a great deal of green water over the top. We were almost blinded by the salt carried in on the stinging lash of spray. The gale made it impossible to stream the sweeps astern so it put an end to further minesweeping. Thankfully, the trawlers made for harbour.

The fact that we could not continue with the sweeping made no difference to my investigation. I already had all the evidence necessary to explain what had been happening on the Humber.

The magnetic field of the Double-ell sweep had been designed to detonate any enemy magnetic mine operating on a sensitivity of .06 of a gauss, the sensitivity the Germans had been using since our first recovery of their magnetic mines. The strength of the magnetic field was greatest towards the end of the sweep cables farthest from the ship, and it gradually lessened until at a point approximately abeam of the sweepers themselves the power of the field was down to .02 of a gauss.

I had brought with me a diagram showing these lines of force in detail, so it had been possible to note where each explosion had occurred in relation to the magnetic field exerted by our Double-ell sweeps. Since the explosions had all taken place within the area of diminishing magnetic strength exerted by the sweeps, it was clear that the Germans had increased the sensitivity of their mines by more than half. Adjustments could be made to protect the minesweepers from this danger.

As for the apparent mystery of channels which had been swept clear of mines becoming alive again, the explanation did not seem hard to guess: among the mines laid there must have been some fitted with the period delay mechanism which we had named the "clicker" after its discovery by Captain Maitland-Dougall when he searched among the debris of an exploded mine during the London blitz. Proof that this was so came when one of the troublesome new mines was recovered and made safe. And, at least, we had now found how the sweepers could themselves be afforded greater protection.

I returned to the Admiralty, reluctant to leave Romyn and his crews but glad to have had the opportunity to go to sea with them.

As for Romyn, the moment the gale had sufficiently abated for him to stream his sweeps astern he was out clearing the channels again. By Christmas Eve that year, the *Rolls Royce* swept her hundredth mine. She was the first minesweeper in history to reach this total and finished the war as the champion sweeper of them all.

Chapter 10

We Hunt the Enemy

We were always faced with the problem of trying to find out how the Germans swept our mines. The reason was, of course, that, if we could discover this, steps could be taken to stop them, and the unswept mines would continue to imperil their shipping. By what precise means our intelligence obtained the first clue to the information we required, I cannot say, but one story was that a German seaman, relaxing too enthusiastically in a waterside bar at one of the occupied European ports, let out the fact that fitted in the bows of his ship was "a whacking great lump of iron, a kind of huge magnet".

An intelligence agent who picked up this information transmitted it to London. We in DTMI came to hear about it. Little deduction was required to realise the significance of the tipsy seaman's indiscretion: his ship was obviously equipped to destroy our magnetic mines laid in enemy waters.

Sometime after this, German documents were captured which mentioned a type of ship called a *Sperrbrecher*, literally "barrier-breaker". This was the name that had been given to the mine-destructor ships.

Even before we had this confirmation we had suspected the nature of the vessels used by the enemy to destroy our magnetic mines. The Royal Navy, working on the assumption that German mines would operate on the same principle as our own, had developed a type of ship to destroy them. H.M.S. *Borde* was the first of these. When the German magnetic mines were discovered to operate on a vertical magnetic field instead of a horizontal field as did ours, a safer and surer method of destroying them than was possible with the *Borde*-type ships had to be evolved; this proved to be the Double-ell sweep. But it was not unreasonable to suppose that the German solution to our magnetic mines should be similar to our original mine-destructor ships.

From what the German seaman had let slip about the magnetic device fitted in the bows of his ship, we could deduce its method of operation. In the crudest and most simple terms, the magnetic device would emit lines of magnetic force ahead of the ship. These would curve down into the water until they met the bottom, then they would travel back through the sea bed, re-emerging to complete the circuit of the magnetic field. It was as if the ship was steaming along on a vast magnetic ellipse. When the magnetic field reached a mine, it would explode it ahead of the ship.

We passed the information we had to the scientists working on mine design, and one of them said: "If you could discover the strength of the magnetic field of the *Sperrbrecher*, we could design a mine that would knock out the ship. Instead of exploding ahead of the vessel, it would go off right underneath her keel."

With this prospect to encourage us, we determined to get the facts the scientists would require. Intelligence agents in France and Belgium were asked to make every possible effort to discover the secrets of the *Sperrbrechers*. Captured seamen were questioned closely. Gradually, more information accumulated about these vessels.

The magnet and electrified coil which they carried in the bows was between four and six hundred *tons* in weight. To accommodate this enormous piece of equipment, a vessel of substantial size was necessary. *Sperrbrechers* were generally around 10,000 to 14,000 tons displacement and upwards of four hundred feet in length. To protect the ships against the possibility of mines exploding too close, the hulls were specially reinforced; and to prevent their sinking; should they suffer damage the holds were filled with empty casks and drums as an extra reserve of buoyancy. The ships were well-equipped with anti-aircraft weapons and were used as convoy escorts and to escort U-boats safely out into deep waters. They were in service from the Baltic down to the Bay of Biscay.

From these facts it was obvious that the *Sperrbrecher* must be proving a most costly necessity to the enemy, who were known to be badly off for vessels of this size. Our mine-laying activities were clearly keeping tied up an enormous tonnage which could much more profitably have been used as freighters or even as armed merchant raiders. We were not, however, merely concerned with straining the enemy's resources in this fashion: we were out to sink the *Sperrbrechers*.

But still the crucial information eluded us.

"The trouble is that you've set us a pretty tall order," said one of the intelligence officers with whom I discussed the problem. "Our people are doing what they can, but I don't hold out a lot of hope. They can get into conversation with the odd seaman in a bar, and when he's in his cups he might let something slip, as the chap did who talked about the 'whacking great lump of iron' in the bows of his ship. But he's hardly likely to blurt out what the magnetic field of the electrified coil is. The chances are that he won't know, anyway. After all, apart from being secret, it's highly technical. Possibly the only way we should find the answer is if one of the German technicians turned traitor and gave it to us."

There were many people in occupied Europe – and in Germany itself – bitterly opposed to the Nazi regime; any of them would gladly have done anything in his power to bring about its downfall. But an act of calculated treachery by a serving member of the German Navy was a different matter; we could not bank on that.

Incidentally, an extraordinary example of the risks that people in Germany were prepared to take to show their detestation of the regime came to light in 1941. An enemy mine which had been recovered and made safe was being stripped down for the usual dissection by our experts. When they examined the magnetic section of the weapon, however, they found that the mine had been perfectly harmless all the time; the firing unit had not been wired up. And then it was discovered how very deliberate this failure had been; painted inside the shell of the mine was the Star of David and in English the words "We are with you!" Under the very noses of foremen and overseers in a German munitions factory, a man had risked his life, first to make sure that the mine would never go off, and secondly to proclaim in the most dangerous way conceivable his hatred for the Nazis. It was such an amazing piece of sabotage that it was brought to the notice of the Prime Minister, and it was suggested that it should be mentioned in broadcasts to the German people to encourage the dissentients. But Churchill ordered the matter to be kept strictly secret. His view was that if Hitler learned about the act of sabotage, the result might be a savage and indiscriminate slaughter of slave labourers forced to work for the Reich.

As for our efforts to find out more about the *Sperrbrecher*, we made no further progress. Eventually, we gave up hope that we should ever succeed.

And then in July, 1942, chance favoured us. A Royal Air Force observer in a reconnaissance aircraft flying nearly three miles high happened quite fortuitously to press the button of his camera at a particular moment on sighting enemy ships. As a result of our liaison with the R.A.F., we had an arrangement that they would send us any photographs taken by their aircraft which they thought might be of interest to us. And so this particular photograph, taken on a routine flight over the enemy naval base at Lorient, in occupied France, was passed to us for information by R.A.F. Station, Medmenham.

Captain Maitland-Dougall began to study it, and after a few moments he said: "Look here, Lincoln, this is vitally important."

On the photograph, taken from 15,000 feet, were three ships. One was a vessel of considerable size, and two were quite small. The two small ships were towing magnetic mine sweeps arranged in diamond formation. In the photograph they were well to the left of the bigger vessel, which was identified in the accompanying typewritten interpretation report from the photographic experts at Medmenham as *Sperrbrecher A.I.*.

The wake of the *Sperrbrecher* showed clearly in the print. Not far from the stern of the ship there was a distinct semicircular patch of disturbed water merging with the V-shaped wake. The cause of this disturbance on the surface of the sea had been the explosion of a mine. According to the R.A.F. photographic experts, the mine was presumed blown up by one of the two small minesweepers.

"That is impossible," said Maitland-Dougall. "See how far they are away. They aren't even on a course that would make it possible. Get on to the R.A.F. and ask them to check on their interpretation. I'm sure it was the *Sperrbrecher* that exploded the mine."

I telephoned Medmenham and pointed out to the photographic interpretation section why Maitland-Dougall disagreed with their findings. They agreed to make a further assessment of the facts presented by the photograph and let us know the outcome. Their second thoughts turned out to tally exactly with what Maitland-Dougall had originally deduced.

Their report was as follows:

> This photograph shows minesweeping in progress off the north-west point of the Ile de Groix, which lies to the south west of the estuary leading to Lorient.
>
> The large vessel is *Sperrbrecher Sp.A.I.* (435 feet). She has been seen in the vicinity for some months and seems to patrol the area between Brest, Ile de Groix and Lorient. She is proceeding at low speed (about six knots) on a course of 55 degrees about 1,500 yards from the island.
>
> At the time of the photograph she is seen to be about two hundred yards *ahead* of the disturbance caused by an explosion in the water which is probably due to a mine. The waves caused by the explosion have radiated to a

distance of about 350 yards from the disturbance which is itself subsiding. Therefore, the explosion must have taken place when the vessel was approaching the spot.

The track of the vessel can be seen in the water, and if she had continued on a straight course she would have passed through the centre of the disturbance. However, she has turned slightly to port and the track passes through the edge of the circle caused by the explosion, consequently disturbing its outline.

Ground reports have indicated that the *Sperrbrechers* have been fitted with anti-mine devices, but there is no evidence of apparatus for this purpose visible on the photographs.

On the same photograph two small vessels, 150 yards apart, are proceeding on a course of 235 degrees towing magnetic sweeps arranged in diamond fashion. They are sweeping in deep water in the channel to the north west of the island where minesweeping has been observed on several other occasions.

Now that Maitland-Dougall's deduction had been confirmed, we knew that the photograph – the first ever to show a *Sperrbrecher* just after detonating a mine – contained all the evidence which we had unsuccessfully attempted for so long to obtain. The detailed collation of the evidence was largely carried out by photographic experts at Air Ministry. Their task was to assist us to find out the position of the mine in relation to the *Sperrbrecher* at the time of the explosion. This was determined most ingeniously.

From their minelaying records and the fact that the precise position of the explosion had been established, the R.A.F. could state quite definitely that the mine involved contained an explosive charge of 740 pounds. The chart showed the depth of water where the explosion occurred was eleven fathoms.

Although we had seen only one of them, a series of photographs had in fact been taken from the reconnaissance aircraft. The period of time covered by the photographic record was seven-and-a-half seconds. Measurement of the ripples of the explosion – no easy matter – showed that these had travelled seventy feet during the seven-and-a-half seconds. That is, at just under ten feet per second. The distance from the centre of the explosion to the outermost ripple measured 1,400 feet. Therefore, the explosion had occurred a second or two under two-and-a-half minutes before the final photograph was taken.

To establish the position of the ship when the mine blew up, her speed had to be known precisely. The photographic experts scaled the spacing of the waves in the ship's wake as shown by each successive photograph, using the wave motion system devised by the late Lord Kelvin, and from this they were able to say that the *Sperrbrecker* was steaming at between six and seven knots.

From the age of the explosion and the speed of the ship it was estimated that the mine had been detonated between 450 and 525 feet ahead of the *Sperrbrecher's* bows. This was a useful guide, but it was not definite enough for our scientists. They had to know much more accurately to be able to determine the strength of the ship's magnetic field; the smallest error could have put them very far out. Naval technical experts tried to calculate more exactly the distance from the ship at which the explosion occurred, but the fact that the *Sperrbrecher* had not kept a straight course added an extra complication, and eventually it was accepted that it was impossible to guarantee that the calculations were precise enough for the design of a mine which would go off under the *Sperrbrecher*.

The only way to be sure was to check the findings and confirm them by specially-staged explosions. The best way to make the check was to have the detonations photographed from directly overhead. The one type of aircraft from which this could be done was an autogyro – helicopters were then still in their infancy. Unfortunately, no autogyro was available. It took nearly twelve months and all the efforts of Maitland-Dougall to get an aircraft put at our disposal. I was sent down to *Vernon* to help arrange the experiments.

As we had a surplus of German mines at *Vernon* which had been recovered and made safe, we decided to use two of the enemy "A"-type rather than expend any of our own. We took the mines out to sea at night to avoid the possibility of Luftwaffe interference.

There was a bit of a swell running, and swinging the mines over the side by derrick proved a tricky operation. If one of the great, ungainly things had swung back inboard and crashed on deck, the consequences might have been most unpleasant. The pair were laid off at Portsmouth, one in five fathoms, the other in ten. Their position was buoyed, and they were wired to the shore so that they could be electrically detonated when the autogyro was directly overhead and ready to take the photographs next day.

From these photographs and from others showing the wakes of vessels under way, the scientists were able to make the necessary checks on the original calculations and build up enough data to assess with extreme accuracy the strength of the magnetic field of the *Sperrbrecher*.

A number of special magnetic mines were designed and manufactured. Minelaying aircraft of Bomber Command flew out to lay these in the patrol area of *Sperrbrecher A.I.* Reconnaissance aircraft kept a special watch for results. We waited to learn if we had been on the right track. It did not take long for confirmation. Within a fortnight of the special mines being laid, *Sperrbrecher A.I.* was blown up on one of them.

The use of large merchant ships as mine-destructors was costly to the enemy; now it could be made still more costly. In every field laid by the Navy and the R.A.F. thenceforward, a proportion of special mines was included. By the end of the war more than a hundred *Sperrbrechers* had fallen victim to the magnetic mines they had gone out to sweep.

Chapter 11

The First Japanese Torpedoes

Generally speaking, Captain Maitland-Dougall and I would arrive for duty at the Admiralty about 9 a.m. each day. Our section was manned day and night, and if anything of particular urgency arose during our absence the night duty officer could always call either of us at our home telephone numbers. When the information arriving overnight was routine, the duty officer would collect together the signals and have them ready for us on our arrival. By this time, in the room adjoining our own which was occupied by the officers of the staff, the charting officer would have charted any minelaying which had taken place. Maitland-Dougall and I could see at once exactly what the situation was, and, if there were reports of mines or unidentified objects around the coast which required special investigation, our officers would be detailed to go to deal with them.

Once this was done, Maitland-Dougall and I would go to our room to study the mass of intelligence reports sent on from other departments. We would pass comments on the dockets attached to the reports offering our explanations and suggestions where these might be helpful.

One report received in the winter of 1941 shocked us profoundly, as, indeed, the news it contained shocked the whole free world when it came to be known: this was the loss of the battleship *Prince of Wales* and the battle-cruiser *Repulse*. But apart from shock over what was unquestionably one of the greatest naval disasters of the war, we were also completely mystified.

121

There was no mystery, of course, about the action itself. The two vessels were steaming with a destroyer escort in north-eastern Malayan waters to attack Japanese transports which were landing troops at the Krau Isthmus. On December 10th, 1941, they were themselves attacked by Japanese high-level and torpedo bombers. The action opened at 11.15 a.m., and in a few minutes over the hour both ships had been sunk.

In the bombing, which was carried out from seventeen thousand feet, the *Repulse* was hit, but it was not the bombs which brought disaster: this was due to the torpedoes.

The *Repulse*, 33,250 tons, was a warship of 1916 vintage, but she had been reconditioned and modernised; she had, moreover, anti-torpedo blisters which were twelve feet thick. During the action she managed to avoid nineteen of the torpedoes launched against her. Yet the five which struck proved fatal.

The *Prince of Wales* was one of Britain's newest battleships and had, in fact, been completed for less than nine months at the time of her sinking. In every way, therefore, she represented the most up-to-date thought in warship design and construction; there was not in the Royal Navy a battleship better able to account for herself. The second torpedo to score a hit on the *Prince of Wales* struck the stern and put the steering gear out of action and damaged her propellers. This left the battleship incapable of taking evasive action. Three more torpedoes, one amidships and two aft, sent her to the bottom.

The mystery lay not in what had happened but how such devastating results had been achieved against such powerful ships by comparatively few torpedoes. Either the Japanese airmen had been exceptionally lucky – and it seemed unlikely that twice in the space of a few minutes they should have had such luck – or they had the most exceptional torpedoes.

At DTMI it became our business to try to discover the answer. Since the United States Navy was operating in the Pacific in far greater force than the Royal Navy, it seemed that the Americans would be more likely to recover Japanese underwater weapons than we should. As we had quite a close working liaison with the U.S. Navy in London, we asked the Americans to let us have, at the earliest opportunity, any information they could obtain on Japanese torpedoes or mines. They promised that the moment they obtained any information of any kind they would pass it on to us.

For two years we heard nothing further.

And then, about the end of January, 1944, a lieutenant of the R.N.V.R., who had been one of our R.M.S.O.s – Rendering Mines Safe Officers – with the Far Eastern Fleet, came into my office at the Admiralty. He said that on his way back from the Pacific he had seen, at the U.S. Navy base in San Diego, California, eight Japanese torpedoes. These had been captured by the Americans on one of the islands of the Pacific. He himself was not a torpedo specialist, and he had not had any opportunity to examine them, but he felt he ought to pass on the information to us at DTMI as he knew how vitally interested we were in all enemy underwater weapons.

The torpedoes, he added, had been at San Diego for a *year!*

Immediately I got in touch with the U.S. Naval Attaché in London, recounted to him these facts and asked: "Why have we not had any information about these Japanese torpedoes?"

"I can't answer that," he said, "but I will signal Washington to find the answer."

The reply that came from Washington was: "No, repeat no, Japanese torpedoes so far recovered."

Our man from the Pacific was able to identify the actual warehouse at San Diego where he had seen the torpedoes, and this information was passed to the U.S. Naval Attaché, who in turn transmitted it to Washington. Some days later a reply came from Washington saying, in effect: "Sorry, nobody told us they were there."

Such a situation, we felt, would not have arisen in the Royal Navy.

The next step was to apply for permission for me to go to the United States to examine and report upon the torpedoes. This was given without hesitation by the Americans, who said I could go as soon as an air passage was available. However, enquiries I made at the Admiralty and at the War Office suggested that the chances of getting a seat in an aircraft without waiting several weeks were quite remote. There were so many V.I.P.s crossing the Atlantic, it seemed, that I could do no more than wait my turn.

The war in the Pacific appeared as though it would continue for some considerable time. It would be bitterly fought. This seemed sufficient reason to me for our knowing without further delay all we possibly could about the Japanese weapons which would be used against Allied naval vessels. In the circumstances, a wait of five or six weeks for a seat in an aircraft did not seem justified.

I found out that the United States Army Air Force had an office in New Quebec Street, by Marble Arch, where there was a colonel who had charge of the allocation of seats in aircraft making the Atlantic crossing. I went to see him. The following conversation ensued:

"Colonel, can we be overheard?"

"No," he said, rising to close carefully all the doors in the room. "You can speak to me in complete confidence."

"Colonel, do you value the lives of your boys in the Pacific?"

"I sure do, Commander."

I explained the situation to him, and said: "It is absolutely vital that I examine these Japanese torpedoes at the earliest possible moment. I sincerely believe that this is a life-or-death matter for your boys in the Pacific."

Three days later, much to the surprise of everyone at the Admiralty, I was in an aircraft bound for the United States. As it was, from the time we had learned of the existence of the Japanese torpedoes, a full month had passed in communications between London, Washington and San Diego, and it was now the beginning of March.

We flew from London to Prestwick, then to Reykjavik, the Icelandic capital, where we should have to wait until darkness fell before taking off again. This was in order that we could continue the Atlantic crossing under cover of night to avoid the attentions of German long-range Focke-Wulf Condors which were ranging the northern skies and would have made short work of an unarmed transport such as ours.

My seat in the aircraft was right in the tail, close by the door. The forward seats were occupied by a general and an admiral with their attendant staffs. As soon as the door of the aircraft was opened at Reykjavik, being nearest I stepped out on to the platform at the top of the flight of steps which had been wheeled against the doorway. Below me, I saw that two companies of U.S. infantrymen had been drawn up to form three sides of a hollow square. For a moment I did not realise the purpose of this, and then the officer commanding the troops ordered: "General salute, present arms!"

Obviously they had expected the general to emerge first from the aircraft. I did not know what to do, whether to salute, though clearly the honours were not intended for me, or whether to try to withdraw inconspicuously into the aircraft. Finally I solved the problem by sidling down the steps and scurrying away. If my appearance at the door of the aircraft rather upset the welcome arranged for the general, the U.S. Army did not hold it against me; I was made fully welcome in the mess.

When night fell, we took off for Gander, Newfoundland. Our arrival there about eight next morning was in bitter cold, and there was snow everywhere. We were told we could not fly on to New York, which was to be our next stop, as the weather was too bad. But after breakfast we were all summoned out to learn that the weather conditions were thought to have improved sufficiently to enable us to continue. Over the State of Maine, however, the aircraft iced up and we had to make an emergency landing at a place called Bear Island, a big United States Air Force base just on the American side of the Canadian frontier.

It was typical of the American sense of hospitality that they should find out that I had been a barrister in civil life and arrange that a member of their legal branch should act as my personal host during the stay. He took me to luncheon and then to the cinema in the afternoon. During the performance, my name was flashed on the screen with the announcement that I was wanted at once. Another weather improvement had made it possible for us to take off once again. This time we reached New York and in due course Washington.

The eight captured Japanese torpedoes had meanwhile been sent from San Diego to Indian Head, Maryland, where in forest land by the Potomac River there was a naval magazine. It covered a vast area, and weapons of all sorts were stored there, including German and Italian underwater weapons as well as the Japanese ones I had come to examine. One item in the cache which particularly interested me was an Italian depth charge known as *Apparechiatura G*, which was intended specifically for use against M.T.B.s. It was so designed that when it reached a certain depth, say fifty feet, a hydrostatic control released a weight, causing the depth charge to have positive buoyancy, rise to the surface and explode. As with so many Italian weapons, it was intended to shake off pursuit and make possible a safe and speedy withdrawal. I had first heard of it in the Mediterranean the previous year. I had vainly searched Sicily and Taranto to try to get hold of a specimen, and ultimately heard that there was one in Sardinia. But when I arrived there the Italians told me that they had already handed it over to the U.S. Navy. When we received no report about it from the Americans, we asked them about it. They replied that they had no trace of the depth charge. Yet here it was at Indian Head. It appeared that, unlike the Royal Navy, they had very little idea of what was in their possession, and this was the explanation of the extraordinary oversight regarding the Japanese torpedoes.

At Indian Head I was entertained by Commander Darrah, who was in command of the magazine, and his wife. They had a house in the middle of the magazine area, and they were exceedingly hospitable. Another U.S. Navy officer, Lieutenant Amesbury, joined me in the investigation.

I should say that the Japanese torpedoes were, mechanically, the finest in the world. They were very simply constructed. The Japanese had used practically no welding and had fitted the parts together by a sort of bayonet joint. Unlike the British torpedoes, or, indeed, those of any Western navy, which were designed to have an almost unlimited number of runs, the Japanese engines had a strictly limited life. In fact, basically, the engines were designed for one practice run and one war run. This was very realistic of the Japanese, since it was all that was really necessary, and it meant that the engines could be much cheaper and more easily constructed. But it was in the mechanism that the Japanese were so far ahead of the rest of the world. They had worked out a means of using oxygen instead of compressed air, and this created a much more powerful explosion of the diesel fuel in the engine. They had also managed to use seawater as a diluent, and this made unnecessary the bottle of distilled water normally found in torpedoes. Since the bottle weighed several hundred pounds, it limited the size of the explosive charge in Western torpedoes to five hundred pounds. By saving the weight of the distilled-water bottle, the Japanese were able to increase their charges by more than half as much again.

The much larger and more destructive warheads explained the sinking of the *Prince of Wales* and *Repulse*. There was now no mystery as to how these two ships should so swiftly have fallen victim to aerial torpedo attack.

With Amesbury, I worked out a drill for rendering safe the pistols of the Japanese torpedoes and recorded all the technical details, including the meaning of the ideographs on the casing which distinguished the different types. The torpedoes were then despatched to Newport, Rhode Island, where we went along for trials at the torpedo experimental station.

The performance of the Japanese torpedoes was quite phenomenal. Their speed was forty-five knots (more than fifty miles per hour), compared with the forty knots maximum for the torpedoes used by other navies. And whereas other torpedoes would run three miles at forty knots, or five miles at thirty knots, the faster Japanese torpedoes ran no less than fifteen miles at top speed.

While I was working at Rhode Island, an American admiral asked: "Why are you British so interested in the performance of enemy weapons? What difference does it make to you?"

I recalled the battle of Midway Island, when, according to account, "the sea was alive" with Japanese torpedoes and enemy destroyers were launching a hundred torpedoes at a time from a distance of close on fifteen miles.

And I said: "Two American cruisers had their bows blown off by Japanese torpedoes. If the cruisers had known they could expect a torpedo attack from that range, they could have taken avoiding action. They would not have been lost."

"So what? We lost two cruisers," said the admiral. "We can build six more."

"But can you train six crews as quickly as that?"

"We'll get by."

During the stay at Rhode Island something happened which seemed to me to supply its own commentary on this attitude of unquestioning confidence in American technological ability.

The Americans had asked us to pass on to them any technical problems which we found we could not overcome. This offer was greatly appreciated because of the enormous burden which the war had imposed upon our resources. One of our problems was to design a torpedo which could be dropped from an aircraft flying at a reasonably safe height. To get satisfactory results from our existing torpedoes, the attacking aircraft had to make their run in from very low altitudes, a hundred feet or less; if they flew higher, the torpedoes either nose-dived or broke up with the force of impact on the water. But the very low-level attack exposed the aircraft to savage retaliation from anti-aircraft fire. A torpedo which could be launched satisfactorily from a relatively safe height of two to three thousand feet would, therefore, afford substantial protection to the lives of torpedo-bomber crews.

At Rhode Island I was told that the high-level torpedo designed by the Americans was ready, and I asked to see the data on the trial results.

The reply was: "You can see anything you like, including the weapons, but no trial results. We have made no trials. We've gone into production straight off the drawing board."

Such was their confidence in the success of the high-level torpedoes that they offered to put on a demonstration right there. With an admiral of the U.S. Navy, I stood on the floating target and prepared to watch the results.

We saw the aircraft flying towards us at between two and three thousand feet. We saw the torpedo leave the aircraft and drop, glistening in the sun, down towards the water. We saw it enter the water with a colossal splash. But we saw no more of it after that; it vanished completely.

Six times the aircraft flew over, six times it launched a torpedo, and six times the torpedo disappeared completely and utterly.

I found it an acutely embarrassing experience, the more so as I had been proudly assured before the demonstration that already they had manufactured a hundred thousand of these torpedoes!

Because of the use to which the knowledge I had obtained on Japanese underwater weapons could be put in the battle going on in the Pacific, the Admiralty decided that I should join the Far Eastern Fleet. A request for me to be allowed to cross America to San Diego, and from there to proceed to join units of the British fleet, was put to Washington. It went to Admiral King, the American Commander-in-Chief, and it was he personally who refused to grant me permission to go to the Pacific. King, who was anti-British, seemed to regard the Pacific as an entirely American concern, wanting neither British ships nor British personnel there if he could help it.

Towards the end of May, while I was hanging around waiting to see if there might be any solution to this peculiar impasse, an urgent signal arrived from London ordering me to return at once to the Admiralty. I reported to the Naval Mission in New York, where I was advised to go by overnight train to Montreal. There I was given a seat in a Liberator, and next day at 7 a.m. I arrived at Prestwick. The weather was too bad for further flying, so I caught the first train south.

When I reported to the duty officer at DTMI, he said: "Come on, Lincoln, we're waiting for you to invade France!"

This greeting, which, of course, was made as a joke, was the first intimation I had that the D-Day landings were only a few days off. But it was not long before I found myself on the Normandy beach-heads.

Chapter 12

The Seine Bay Invasion Mystery

A signal received at the Admiralty after the Normandy landings from the Flag Officer of the British Assault Area sent me flying off on August 13, 1944, to a stretch of the French coast known by the code name of "Juno" Area, where I was to be confronted with a problem as puzzling as any we had been called upon to solve.

On three successive mornings prior to my receiving the summons, explosions had occurred inside the artificial Mulberry harbour at "Juno" Area, and on each occasion a ship had been damaged. The victim of the attack on the first morning was a cruiser, H.M.S. *Frobisher*, on the second morning a supply ship, the S.S. *Iddesleigh*, on the third a depot ship, H.M.S. *Albatross*.

Inside the breakwaters of a Mulberry harbour, these vessels should have been safe, at least from underwater attack. The fact that they could be picked off, one after the other as they lay at anchor, showed that the Germans, even though in retreat, were still using all their ingenuity to delay the day of defeat. The theory was that they had brought a new underwater weapon into operation. My task was to discover what the weapon was and how it could be countered.

Already I had visited "Juno" Area after the Normandy landings to investigate new types of mines – including the oyster mine – which the Germans had used, and so I was at least familiar with the local geography.

As the aircraft in which I was flying crossed Seine Bay, it was possible to see away to the east the hazy outline of the Seine Estuary, where the enemy were still in occupation; far away to the west was the Cherbourg Peninsula; and right ahead was "Juno" Area. From above, the Mulberry harbour looked protective enough to ensure the safety of the ships inside. Indeed, it was difficult to see how an underwater attack could have been made.

At the western end, running out more or less at right angles from the shore were the big caissons sunk to form the quay for unloading the supply ships. At the seaward end, running at right angles to the caissons, was a row of sunken ships. The narrow gap between the ships and caissons was the entrance to the harbour. At the eastern end, the stretch of water between the sunken ships and the shore was crossed by a stout net of steel mesh supported by buoys.

Looking down on the ships at anchor inside this most impressive combination of pre-fabrication and improvisation, I could not help thinking of the last time a comparable situation had arisen. This had been in the previous September at Taranto, shortly after the Italian base fell. As with the three ships attacked at "Juno" Area, a moored vessel had been involved. H.M.S. *Abdiel*, a fast minelaying cruiser, blew up with the loss of all but thirty lives. It was a most ghastly tragedy, for in addition to her crew she carried six hundred paratroops below decks. At first it was thought that the disaster had been caused by a mine; but no one could understand why this had not gone off earlier, as the *Abdiel* had been moored for twelve hours before the explosion came at midnight.

In the naval magazine ashore, I found dozens of curious wooden objects like large wheels. These had been segmented to form a number of compartments. The Germans had put depth charges into the compartments of some of these "wheels" which were fitted with clocks which could be set to cause a central charge to explode at any pre-determined period ranging from fifteen minutes to twenty-four hours. This in turn exploded the surrounding charges consisting of something like 2,000 pounds of high explosives. The Germans had sunk some "wheels" near buoys around the harbour before they withdrew, and one of them undoubtedly blew up the *Abdiel*.

There was, of course, a very different situation at "Juno" Area from that of Taranto: the Mulberry harbour had been built since the Germans were driven from that stretch of the Seine Bay coast, and they could not possibly have left booby traps capable of operating after this lapse of time. Anyway, there was no point in arriving with a preconceived idea of what might have happened; I had to approach the problem with a completely open mind and wait till I had gathered all the facts before trying to reach any conclusion.

At 18:30, I reported to the Flag Officer of the British Assault Area, who had his headquarters in a great tented camp close by the harbour, and during the evening he, his Chief-of-Staff and his Torpedo Officer gave me a complete picture of the situation.

The one incontestable fact was that the damage to the three ships had been caused by contact explosions, but beyond that there seemed to be no evidence on which to reach any further conclusions. There was a wide range of possible theories as to how the underwater weapons responsible for the damage were introduced into the anchorage. The one explanation which did not seem possible was that torpedoes had been used; no enemy vessels had approached close enough to fire these, even if they could have been got through the defences. Perhaps the most obvious way to get an explosive device, say an aerial torpedo, into the harbour would be to plant it there by aircraft, but there had been no aerial activity reported to link with the three morning explosions. Another possibility seemed to be that frogmen could have got through the defensive wire net at the eastern end of the harbour and fixed limpet mines to the ships. But the nearest enemy position along the coast was too far to allow frogmen to swim that distance, nor was there any radar report of enemy vessels approaching sufficiently close to bring frogmen within range; and even if they could have reached the harbour, there was still the problem of their escape: there had been no sign of frogmen anywhere nearby.

If the radar reports seemed to exclude the use of either torpedoes or frogmen, they showed nonetheless a very interesting situation.

At 3:15 a.m. on August 9th, a flotilla of German E-boats had been observed on the radar screen leaving the mouth of the River Seine. The nearest they came to "Juno" Area was a distance of twenty-two miles. They returned again at 4.45 a.m. without apparently having done anything to justify their putting to sea at all.

The *Frobisher* explosion occurred at 7.17 a.m.

In the early hours of the following morning, the E-boats were out again. The nearest their tracks came to "Juno" Area on this occasion was a distance of eighteen miles. This time they left the mouth of the Seine at around 4 a.m. and returned an hour later.

The *Iddesleigh* explosion occurred at 6.35 a.m.

The overnight radar report preceding the third explosion on August 11th was not quite as clear as had been the two earlier ones. E-boats were known to have been operating from the mouth of the Seine briefly around 1.30 a.m., but on this occasion they were observed only for a matter of twenty minutes. Later they reappeared about 3 a.m., coming within twenty-one miles of "Juno" Area, but for some reason radar detection was imperfect and the exact duration of this sortie could not be established.

The *Albatross* explosion occurred at 7 a.m.

Three times, on successive nights, the enemy had thought fit to send out E-boat flotillas. Within four hours of the flotillas being tracked on the radar screen, a ship anchored in the Mulberry harbour had fallen victim to a mysterious explosion. The activities of the E-boats and the subsequent happenings in the anchorage seemed more than a coincidence. Either the patrols had been utterly aimless, or they were connected in some way with the explosions.

And then came a vital and quite unexpected piece of evidence which upset all our reasoning as to the nature of the weapon that was being used. Aboard the *Albatross* I found a piece of metal from the explosion. It was undoubtedly part of a German torpedo warhead.

I said in my report at the time to the Admiralty:

> This points to the weapon being some kind of torpedo. The use of E-boats, which are fitted with torpedo tubes, makes the use of some form of torpedo probable. It is also significant that the attacks were carried out from a position and at a time when good use would be made of the strong west-going tide. All hits were contact hits and it is unlikely that the enemy would use a speed of less than six knots if the weapon is, in fact, some form of torpedo, since this speed would be the minimum at which a contact pistol would be certain to fire, and too low a speed would make depth-keeping impossible.
>
> From the above facts it seems reasonable to assume that the weapon in question is a long-range torpedo capable of covering a distance of some twenty-five to thirty miles, which is being fired as a browning shot into the ships in the anchorage in "Juno" Area.
>
> The torpedo is apparently slow-running since it takes approximately four hours to cover distances of twenty to twenty-five miles, and use has to be made of the additional assistance afforded by the west-going tide. Judging from the damage to *Frobisher* and *Albatross* the torpedo is set to a depth of approximately ten feet.
>
> It is possible that the torpedo is set to circle or zig-zag through the anchorage, that is to say after a pre-set run, but there is at present no evidence of this. It is difficult to judge from three cases only, but it is significant that all the ships were struck on the port – that is, the seaward – side.

It struck me that if advantage was being taken of the west-going tide and ships were lying bows on to the tide, as they would be in the absence of high wind, that the best chance of a hit would be obtained by zig-zagging or circling torpedo. All hits being on the port side, however, seemed to point to attacks coming from one direction only.

Accordingly, I arranged to be taken out in a boat to the anchorage in order to observe the behaviour of the ships on the west-going tide. I found that off Courseulles the west-going tide flows in fact from south-east to north-west owing to the configuration of the coast, so that at the time of the attacks the ships struck would have been presenting a good target to anyone firing from the mouth of the Seine. These facts would seem to point to the possibility of the weapon being merely a long, slow-running straight torpedo.

It is strange that none of these weapons have so far come ashore, but explosions have been reported on the bottom at the same time as the attacks on the *Frobisher*, and so many explosions take place in the Seine Bay area that ships have ceased to report them as being in any way unusual occurrences.

During my stay, there was another type of explosion that was uncomfortably frequent. Each night, an eleven-inch gun which was thought to be situated about eighteen miles along the coast, shelled us regularly. It used high velocity missiles which were set to burst in the air over our heads. After each deafening detonation we were showered by great jagged pieces of metal. Since we were under canvas the experience was highly disagreeable. All night long there were frequent cries of "Stretcher bearer!" One morning I awakened to find a large ragged hole in the tent over my head, and close to where I lay was a highly lethal piece of ironmongery which I still keep as a reminder of my extreme good fortune that it landed no nearer. H.M.S. *Erebus* was brought up to deal with this nightly danger, but her difficulty was to locate the gun, which was believed to be mounted on railway waggons and hidden in a tunnel by day. A day or two after my return from the area I noted with considerable pleasure that rocket-firing Typhoons had at last located the menace and dealt with it appropriately.

My deductions on the evidence so far on the mystery explosions in Seine Bay were that they had been caused by torpedoes with something like five times the range of anything we had encountered. This suggested that the Germans had evolved a completely new type of torpedo. After my recent visit to the United States and the discoveries I had made there, the thought crossed my mind that they might have received technical advice from their Japanese allies, but whether now, by adopting Japanese methods of propulsion, the Germans had succeeded in producing a torpedo of prodigious range, it was impossible to say. The only way to find out the nature of their new weapon was to recover a specimen.

There was a report on the night preceding the *Frobisher* attack that a disturbance was observed to be taking place in the net which had been laid as an anti-torpedo protection to the seaward anchorage. It seemed quite likely that one of the new torpedoes had become stranded in the mesh of the net. By this time, owing to heavy weather and the strong tidal streams, the net afforded little protection, and it was intended in any event to recover and replace it with another. I urged that the net should now be beached for examination to see if we could recover from it one of the new weapons.

The Boom Defence Vessel *Barlake* was set to work recovering the net. Two Bomb Safety Officers, Lieutenant Wooster and Lieutenant Laxton, were on board to deal with any objects that might come to light as the net was raised by the hoisting gear fitted in the *Barlake's* bows. I was in a small boat in by the shore, ready to examine the net as it was beached. Unfortunately, while securing the first part of the net aboard the *Barlake* an explosion occurred; one man was killed, three were seriously injured, and Wooster and Laxton were both slightly injured. The explosion was thought to have been caused by a parachuted circling torpedo which had been caught in the net. The torpedo must have been brought against the ship so that its very sensitive pistol went off, exploding the three-hundred-pound charge. This put an end to *Barlake's* recovery efforts. Further examination of the net suggested that it was full of explosive objects of one kind or another.

The Flag Officer did not wish to risk any of his craft on further recovery operations, so I left for Cherbourg to try to get the *Vernon* Mine Recovery Flotilla, under Lieutenant-Commander Gallieu, to come down to "Juno" Area to beach the net. Meanwhile, new nets were being laid, this time with an overlap, to protect the "Juno" Area anchorage from attacks from the east and north-east. If any more long-range torpedoes were fired from the mouth of the Seine they would not now get through to the anchored vessels.

While I was at Cherbourg, the officer who was clearing the harbour of mines, Lieutenant-Commander Chapple, told me of an object he had discovered which sounded as though it might be the new type of torpedo we were hoping to recover. He had moored it in shallow water on the west side of the Grande Rade and marked it with a dan buoy. We had to go in a small boat to examine the object because, although it was exposed at low water, it was not high and dry. We made our approach cautiously for we were told that a similar object had exploded when being trawled. When to the windward of the object we stopped the boat's engine and drifted down on wind and tide. We were able this way to get very close. But I could see that it was not what I was after: it was not a torpedo but a very large paravane, and it was so rusty that it was impossible to say whether it was French or German.

The weather had become too heavy for the work of recovering the net at "Juno" Area, and the vessels for the job had to wait at Cherbourg for conditions to moderate. Meanwhile, I had to return to London.

When the net was recovered, it contained the catch we were seeking. It proved to be a torpedo all right, but not of the completely new type which I had anticipated. It was driven electrically, and this accounted for the absence of any track such as there would have been if it had been driven by compressed air; if there had been a track, of course, this would have been sighted as the torpedo entered the anchorage, and there would have been no mystery over the explosions.

The explanation of the torpedo's amazingly long range was much simpler than we had expected: what the Germans had in fact done was to weld together the cases of two electric torpedoes so as to get double battery space necessary to carry the warhead up to thirty miles. The speed of this long range torpedo was only about five knots, but by firing it to run with the ebb it would gather the extra knot or two from the west-going tide to give it the necessary speed to cover the distance and explode on contact.

It was a very ingenious weapon, but though it had scored three hits I do not think it could be regarded from the German point of view as a success. How many long-range torpedoes they fired to get their three hits we had no means of knowing; but I imagine the number that went completely astray must have been very large. Our view was that it was a weapon conceived in desperation; the Germans knew they were defeated, that shortly they would have no use for their torpedoes, and so, as a last throw, they had hit on the idea of doubling the range of their torpedoes in the hope that when fired virtually at random they might claim a victim.

Chapter 13

The Discovery of the Acoustic Torpedo

In any intelligence work, the gathering of information tends to be rather indiscriminate. Facts are gathered for their own sake in the hope that when there are enough of them they will point clearly in the direction the enemy is thinking or working. Seldom do all the facts on any particular development come to light at a given moment. Sometimes when a great many facts have been gathered they still do not present a complete and accurate picture, for some vital aspect remains unknown, and conclusions reached without the facts being complete can be widely misleading. Occasionally, as with the *BM 1000 Bombemine*, the whole picture emerges fairly quickly, yet entirely accurately, and the problem is capable of swift solution. At other times, the gathering of facts may take months, or even years, before an investigation is complete.

One such instance arose out of what might be called The Case of the Talkative *Feldwebel*. It began when an interrogation officer telephoned me from Cockfosters one day in the spring of 1941. He sounded almost apologetic. He did not think the information he had to impart was really of much consequence, and he had hesitated to trouble us with it. When I heard what he had to say, I was inclined to agree with him. However, subsequent events proved how wrong we both were.

A *Feldwebel* in Rommel's Afrika Korps had been captured in the Western Desert and brought to this country.

"The interesting thing," said the interrogator, "is that he comes from a little Baltic port near Kiel called Eckernförde."

"That's the place where the Germans have their *Torpedoversuchsanstalt*," I said.

"Exactly. The point is that this German sergeant's father is a foreman at the torpedo research factory."

"Does he himself know anything about torpedoes?"

"There is no reason to suppose he does. We haven't questioned him yet."

On the face of it, the German did not seem a promising prospect. There was no reason for him to know what went on inside his father's factory, at any rate to know the sort of technical details which would interest us.

"What sort of a man is he?"

"He seems an open, straightforward type. He talks very freely. But as he's a soldier and has no personal connections with the sea, it's doubtful, I'd say, that you'll learn anything of value from him."

I, too, felt dubious, but we were so desperate to get any lead on German torpedo development that I did not like to neglect even the remotest opportunity. I told Captain Maitland-Dougall about my conversation with Cockfosters.

"You'd better go out and see the fellow, Lincoln," he said. "We can't really afford to let slip any possible source of information, however unpromising."

So it was arranged that I should meet the talkative *Feldwebel*, and I drove out to Cockfosters but with no very high hopes of the journey producing anything worthwhile.

Before the German was brought into one of the now familiar small, bare interrogation rooms, I primed the interrogating officer with what seemed to me to be the most promising lines of questioning, and then, seated inconspicuously in the corner, I waited to see if anything emerged.

The *Feldwebel* was marched in. He was of medium height and build, with fair hair, blue eyes and a typically Teutonic cast of features. Right from the start, as the interrogator began his oblique approach, it was obvious that the German was a friendly, amiable individual. There was nothing restrained about his manner; he answered the questions put to him quite readily, and, indeed, gave the impression that he was rather pleased to have the opportunity for an informal chat on things in general. The questions were naturally framed in such a way that he would get the impression that there was no more than this involved.

Finally, the interrogator worked round to the subject of the man's family.

"I believe your father is foreman at the torpedo factory at Eckernförde?"

"Yes, sir, that is correct."

"I don't suppose you've ever been allowed to visit the factory when you have been home on leave?"

"Indeed, I have, sir. In fact, I have been out with my father in a boat at night when he was engaged in testing torpedoes."

This sounded distinctly odd to me. I had attended torpedo testings on a number of occasions, and these were always carried out during the day, otherwise we should never have been able to observe the torpedoes. Our tests were made on a Scottish loch chosen because of the clarity of its water. We would stand on the test float and watch the torpedoes rushing straight towards us on a track deep enough to take them safely underneath the float but close enough to the surface for us to be able to see how they were running.

"You did say at night?"

"Yes, sir."

"But how could you see torpedoes being tested in the dark?"

"That was easy, sir. They had a light on the front of them which shone up through the water."

"You mean, that as the torpedo raced along you could watch the light cutting straight through the water?"

"Not straight through the water, sir. The torpedoes weaved from side to side."

This sounded complete nonsense. The whole point of a torpedo was that it should go straight as an arrow for its target.

In fact, every naval power in the world had spent hundreds of thousands of pounds – possibly even millions – perfecting gyroscopes to ensure that their torpedoes ran absolutely straight, without deviation, towards their targets. I thought perhaps I had misunderstood the man; I asked the interrogator to question him more closely on the way the torpedoes travelled.

"They go like this," said the German, making a snaking motion with his hand.

"Draw it on this piece of paper," said the interrogator.

The German drew a wavy line; there was no doubt at all what he wanted to convey.

"It must have been a dud in which the gyro had failed," I said to the interrogator. "Ask him how many torpedoes behaved like this."

"Every torpedo does that," said the *Feldwebel*.

I got the interrogator to question him still more closely, but the *Feldwebel* just could not be shaken from his story.

"Of course, I know nothing about torpedoes myself, sir," he said. "I can only tell you what I have seen with my own eyes. These torpedoes my father tested followed a wavy track."

I set off back to London considerably mystified. Either the German was having us on in a very big way, or he had described a completely revolutionary form of underwater weapon. What I had to try to decide in my own mind was whether or not the man was lying.

It is difficult ever to know what is going on in the mind of another man, and when that man is a foreigner and at the same time an enemy it is even harder to judge. His motives must always be suspect. But then the question occurred to me: what were the *Feldwebel's* motives? Did he in fact have any motives at all, or was he merely a straightforward, uncomplicated man who had talked as he had done because the conversation had been skilfully guided into certain channels without arousing his suspicions, and flattering attention had been paid to what he had said? I recalled his open, honest face; it was hard to imagine any guile there. And I recalled again his words: "I know nothing about torpedoes myself." There seemed to be the answer. He was a soldier, a landsman with no knowledge whatever about naval matters. He had seen torpedoes being tested, but as he had neither special interest in them nor knowledge of them the significance of the tests entirely escaped him. Because he knew nothing about torpedoes himself, he did not for a moment imagine he was telling us anything of any consequence. He had given no technical details because he knew none; he had simply described what he had seen. What harm (he might think, if he gave the matter any thought) could there be in that?

I decided that the *Feldwebel* had been telling the truth and what he had said was of vital significance. On arriving at the Admiralty I reported all that I had learned to Maitland-Dougall.

"I think," he said, "we had better see what Carslake makes of this."

Captain Carslake, R.N., was a most exceptional man. Apart from being a very capable torpedo specialist officer, he enjoyed a considerable reputation outside the Navy as a *savant*. His book advancing the theory that time does not exist but is merely a product of the human imagination had established him as a philosopher of originality. At the first reading of the book, the late Sir Oliver Lodge had confessed that he did not understand it at all; at the second reading he declared that Carslake was a genius.

Maitland-Dougall and I recounted to Carslake the story of the talkative *Feldwebel*.

"This could mean that the Germans have developed an acoustically operated torpedo," said Carslake.

His conclusion was endorsed by the experts in H.M.S. *Vernon*.

The idea of an acoustically directed torpedo was not new. It was something that we had tried to develop ourselves, but without success. The Germans were the ingenious sort of people who might well succeed in such a technically difficult project.

The torpedo would have microphones fitted in the warhead and according to the way these picked up sounds so would the torpedo be guided. If sounds were made to port, it would turn to port; if they were made to starboard, it would turn to starboard. During tests, if sounds were made from alternating quarters, the torpedo would run on a wavy track as the *Feldwebel* had described.

The torpedo would home on to its target by picking up the sound waves emitted by it. A vessel's propeller noises would attract the torpedo to the stern. The experts concluded that the first proof that the Germans were using the new weapon would be when reports came in of ships being torpedoed in the stern.

The implication behind all this was that a U-boat fitted with acoustic torpedoes could take up any position abeam or astern of a convoy and fire almost at random. After that, the propeller noises of the ships would ensure their destruction. A U-boat pack equipped with these weapons could attack the largest of our convoys and not only sink the merchantmen but also the escort vessels which, owing to their greater speed, were ordinarily almost immune from successful torpedo attack. Another type of vessel which had so far enjoyed considerable immunity was the fast ocean liner which usually steamed unescorted and depended on speed for safety. These ships, including the two Queens, were employed on trooping runs; they often carried thousands of men at a time; now they were threatened. The implications of the acoustic torpedo were horrifying.

Our discovery was reported at once to Naval Staff, who ordered a counter-measure to be prepared. The scientists came back to us to say this could not be done unless they knew the wavelength at which the microphones of the torpedo were designed to operate. We had no means of knowing this. The scientists were asked to work on the basis of covering as far as possible the band of sound waves that would be given off by an ordinary, average merchant ship proceeding at ten knots. Sound measurements were taken to find out the wavelengths of the noises such ships created. A noise box was then designed to produce the necessary volume of sound. It was in fact a development of a Canadian project originally intended as an acoustic minesweep. The idea was that it would be towed astern of a ship and by the noise it made would attract the new German homing torpedo, so diverting it from the ship's propeller.

Since its purpose was to fox, it was given the code name "Foxer". Thousands of "Foxers" were manufactured and stored in readiness. The orders were that they were not to be issued until we had proof that acoustic torpedoes had been used. The only way we should know this would be when reports started coming in of ships being struck in the stern. But, once the alarm was given, we were ready to deal with the threat to our ocean life-lines. We were more prepared to deal with a new underwater weapon – or so it seemed – than ever we had been before.

But the months went by, and nothing happened. The pattern of torpedo attack remained unchanged. There was no sign of any increase in the number of vessels struck in the stern. I began to wonder whether the *Feldwebel* had been less innocent than he appeared to be, whether the lights weaving through the waters of the Baltic had not just been something that he had imagined. Yet he did not seem the type. I was prepared to back my original judgment on the man until definite proof came that I was wrong.

It was about six months after my visit to Cockfosters that, quite suddenly, what appeared to be proof of my error reached Admiralty. Intelligence had received information that the Germans were using a new torpedo called *Fat*. At first it seemed as though it might be the weapon for which we had prepared. But the Cockfosters interrogators discovered from U-boat prisoners that *Fat* did not work acoustically. It in fact zig-zagged, though not in the way the *Feldwebel* had described.

The *Fat* torpedo was designed to run a certain distance, and if by the time it had covered the distance it had not struck a target it turned back on its own course. It continued to do this until it ran out of fuel and sank. The first run it made might take it two-and-a-half miles, and when it turned back on its reciprocal course it might cover half-a-mile, continuing to and fro in runs of half-a-mile all the time its fuel remained.

The purpose of such a torpedo was clear. A U-boat had only to take up position on the beam of an approaching convoy and fire its *Fat* torpedoes at the leading ship. If they overran the target without scoring a strike, they would run back into the convoy, doubling to and fro across the columns of merchantmen until they found victims. As the average Atlantic convoy covered many square miles of sea it seemed hardly possible that a spread of these torpedoes could be fired without hitting some of the vessels. Convoy escorts were warned of the new threat, but there was little that could be done against it.

It looked as if our guess about the acoustic torpedo had been completely wrong. At any rate, this was the accusation made. I was hauled on the carpet by the Director of Torpedoes and Mining and told that I had put the country to a lot of expense – the manufacture of thousands of "Foxers" had been by no means cheap – and that the whole fiasco was due to faulty information on my part that had led to the making of a wild guess.

"We have been made to look fools in the eyes of the Staff," he said. "It must not happen again."

I felt very disheartened. The one thing that made my position tolerable was the sympathetic attitude of Maitland-Dougall. He offered no reproaches.

"Don't you worry about this, Lincoln," he said. "The war is not over yet."

On January 14, 1943, while Mr. Churchill, President Roosevelt and the British and American Chiefs of Staff were meeting at Casablanca to decide the future course of the war, a report came in to the Admiralty. It concerned a fast convoy of six tankers which had left Trinidad with one escort vessel to protect them. As they were speeding through the South Atlantic they had been attacked by a U-boat. All had been torpedoed in the stern.

The *Feldwebel* had not been mistaken. What he had described was in fact the testing of acoustic torpedoes that required no accuracy of aim. With a speed of forty to forty-five knots, these torpedoes could overtake the fastest of ships and be certain to home on to their targets because the victim itself supplied the necessary guidance to ensure its destruction.

Immediately, an instruction went out from Admiralty to all naval authorities at home and abroad: "Issue 'Foxers' to all ships."

Meanwhile, there were warships and merchantmen scattered about the oceans which could not be issued with "Foxers" before they returned to port. One of these was H.M.S. *Lagan*, a frigate escorting a westbound Atlantic convoy. She was attacked by a U-boat using homing torpedoes, and her stern was blown off. This suggested that the U-boats would concentrate on putting escort vessels out of action with acoustic torpedoes, leaving the merchantmen unprotected and completely vulnerable to massacre by ordinary torpedo attack.

But the "Foxer" proved an efficient counter to the new weapon, which was given the code name "Gnat", formed from the initial letters of the words German Naval Acoustic Torpedo.

Although the "Foxer" was effective, there were considerable disadvantages to its use. Captains of ships whose job it was to hunt U-boats complained that when seeking their quarry near to a convoy the din caused by the trailing "Foxers" jammed their asdic sets. We set about trying to find the exact wavelength on which the "Gnat" worked in order to improve the "Foxer" and see if it was possible to overcome its disadvantages.

The ideal way to discover the technical secrets of a weapon was to recover a specimen and dissect it. But it proved impossible to recover a "Gnat". Intelligence agents working in enemy occupied territory had no success either in obtaining the information required. We went to enormous effort, but we failed completely. It was ironic that we should have been put to so much trouble, for it should have been unnecessary. The information we required was in the possession of one of our allies.

The Russians had the good fortune to capture the German submarine *U-250*, which was armed with acoustic torpedoes. One would have thought that our allies would have passed on to us the technical details of the weapon. For reasons best known to themselves, they did not do so. When we asked for the information, the rather vague reply came that we should receive it in due course. Not satisfied with this, we asked if we could send two officers to see the submarine and its torpedoes. A ten-week delay over the granting of visas ensued. This was followed by a laboured discussion with the Russians about the route the officers should take to go to Russia. They were not to be allowed to fly there direct. Finally, they had to go to Persia, from where a Russian aircraft took them to Batum and then to Moscow.

Now, from being infinitely tedious the situation became positively Orwellian. The two officers were shut in separate rooms and confined under close guard. Each was presented with a questionnaire consisting of several hundred questions on the Royal Navy and its weapons. They were told that before anything further could be done they must answer the questions. Both declined to do so. They were informed that they would be kept in Moscow until the answers were given. For weeks we had no news of the officers. Eventually, as a result of urgent signals to the British Naval Attaché in Moscow, their release was secured. They were allowed to continue on their journey to Kronstadt, the Russian fortress island north of Leningrad, where the *U-250* was lying. Their Russian escorts took them to a basin and pointed across to the far side where the vessel was berthed. This, the officers realised, was all they were to be allowed to see of the *U-250*. They protested that they had come to inspect the acoustic torpedoes. "You can see them," said the Russians, pointing to a pile of torpedoes lying on the farther side of the basin. "Now you can go back to England and say you have seen the *U-250* and the torpedoes."

After that, we were relieved merely to see the officers back safely in Britain. There clearly was no point in continuing the efforts to obtain the facts we needed from the Russians; they had made it abundantly clear that they were going to tell us nothing whatever about the "Gnat". We continued with our own efforts.

The months went by. The North African campaign ended in victory for the Allies; Sicily was invaded and fell to British and American forces; Mussolini was toppled from power; Italy surrendered, and a foothold was gained in southern Europe with the Allied landings at Reggio and Salerno.

During the Italian campaign I found further proof that the German *Feldwebel* I had interviewed at Cockfosters had been speaking the truth when he spoke of the night-testing of torpedoes in the Baltic.

In February, 1943, I had to go into hospital for a stomach operation. The doctors said the condition was brought on by the anxiety caused through the work I had been doing; they recommended a change for a while. It so happened that I had heard of a unit known as No.30 Commando which appeared to land itself in interesting situations. It consisted of a body of marines and was commanded by specialist naval officers. I asked Maitland-Dougall if I might join it for "field work" which would offer a change, even if it was not strictly what the doctors had in mind. He agreed, and I joined the Commando in Sicily.

The events of that Mediterranean interlude have no part in this account, and I merely mention it to explain how I happened to be concerned with the capture of the Silurificio Italiano, the Italian torpedo factory at Baia, north of Naples, in 1943. There, among the torpedo stores, I found practice heads with lights fitted to them. Obviously, the Germans had copied the idea from the Italians, and this explained how the *Feldwebel* came to see the light weaving across the surface of the Baltic when he went out in the launch at night to watch acoustic torpedoes undergoing test.

But still we were no nearer the solution of the problems outstanding on the "Gnat".

D-Day brought the invasion of northern Europe, and after weeks of severe fighting came the break-out at Caen and the drive of the Allied armies towards Paris.

At this time, whenever I happened to be in our office at the Admiralty, I found great interest in the Army Intelligence reports covering the advance through France. Whoever was responsible for compiling these reports did not merely content himself with listing the places which had fallen into Allied hands but, in guide book style, mentioned any interesting facts he could find about them. So that instead of simply recording that Bayeux had been taken he went on to add something like this: "Bayeux is the home of the famous tapestry representing in panoramic form the invasion and conquest of England by William of Normandy." Through the eyes of this indefatigable British Army Baedeker, I followed our forces on their way to relieve the French capital. They reached Houilles "... which lies about ten miles north-west of Paris and is a centre of the mushroom industry, the mushrooms being grown in caves outside the village ..."

It was there that I stopped reading. The description of Houilles evoked a response in a remote corner of my memory. The combination of mushrooms and caves seemed suddenly significant. For a while I could not think why, simply having the conviction that it was, and then I remembered that the code word used by the Germans for their torpedo storage depot in Northern France was "Pilz". This is the German for mushrooms. Mushroom caves would be an ideal hiding place for torpedoes, which could be stored deep inside, safe from any possibility of bombing attack.

We had an officer attached to the advanced units of the Army, and I sent a signal asking him to investigate the caves at Houilles to see if there were any torpedoes stored there. It was purely a chance shot, but it came off. His reply was that there were stocks of torpedoes in the caves.

At once I set off by air for France, flying from Croydon to Le Bourget. I was accompanied by a young scientist named Maurice Hills, the son of a Cambridge professor and himself a Cambridge man. He was one of a group of scientists who had been brought into the Navy and given temporary commissions. They wore naval commando uniforms, khaki battle-dress with navy and gold epaulets. The whole party of them were sent up to us at DTMI to be "put into the picture". When we lined them up, we found one of them was wearing a moustache. We told him we were sorry, but if he wanted to remain a naval officer he would have to sacrifice his moustache.

When Hills and I reached Houilles, we met Lieutenant Hughes, R.N.V.R. whom I had signalled, and started to search the mushroom caves. There were a number of air-driven and electric torpedoes, but of the acoustic torpedo which we had hoped to find there was no sign. There were, however, plenty of gaps in the storage racks in the caves.

"The Germans seem to have done their best to destroy stocks before they pulled out," said Hughes. "They piled a lot in a field and blew them up."

We went out to examine the debris. It was scattered over a wide area.

Hughes said: "The gannets have been here, picking up what they could."

By gannets he meant the French Navy; they obviously would want to collect whatever German material they could to examine it, and I decided I would pay them a call in Paris to see if they had recovered anything that might throw light on the "Gnat".

Meanwhile, I poked about in the rubble. Past experience had proved that, however spectacular an explosion, it never quite shattered everything. The fragments that remained were often of great value. Now from the debris that littered the field I found parts of what might have been a wireless set: pieces of wire, portions of transformers and circuits, aluminium strips, pieces of bakelite. It seemed quite certain that these had come from acoustic units of "Gnat" torpedoes. Obviously, Admiral Doenitz had been determined at all costs that, whatever else might be left behind, not a single specimen of his most-prized U-boat weapon must survive intact to fall into our hands. But what we were primarily interested in was the "brain" of the weapon, and there seemed to be enough fragments scattered about the field to make possible a reconstruction of the acoustic unit by the specialists in H.M.S. *Vernon*.

Hill and I went to work. We quartered the whole area on our hands and knees. It was a most laborious job and it kept us busy for several hours, but finally we finished up with three sackfuls of bits and pieces, including two or three tiny microphones, damaged but possibly capable of repair. We borrowed a Humber staff car from an Army unit stationed nearby, loaded into it our hard-won spoils and drove off to Paris.

At the British Embassy the Naval Attaché arranged for me to meet Rear-Admiral Louis Kahn, at the French Ministry of Marine. Kahn had the unusual title for a seaman of "Engineer-General". After France capitulated, he had fallen foul of the Vichy authorities who threw him into jail. He managed to escape and made his way into Spain. He was held there for a time but eventually succeeded in reaching Gibraltar. From there he went on to join the Free French Forces under de Gaulle. Now he was chief of the technical section of the French Navy.

I explained to the admiral what my mission was and how long I had worked to find the secrets of the German acoustic torpedo.

"Some of your people got to Houilles before me," I said. "They have been over the ground and no doubt made the best pickings. I should like to have whatever they found."

"If we help you," said Kahn, "will you share with us the information you gather from this material?"

"I shall certainly repeat your request to my superiors at the Admiralty, sir."

"Then we shall do what we can to help you."

He gave me a chit to a scientist named Lescop in whose possession was the material that had been collected at Houilles. Lescop gave me a valve, an undamaged microphone and some pieces of bakelite.

Now Hills and I were ready to leave Paris. While in the city I had taken the opportunity to buy a ring for my wife whose birthday was approaching. We drove to Le Havre along snow-covered roads, and as soon as we reached the port made inquiries about a passage to Portsmouth. The best we could do, however, was to join an American tank landing ship which that night was leaving in convoy for Portland. We drove our laden staff car straight on to the tank deck. Hills and I were given cabins and we turned in.

It was about 2 a.m. when I was awakened by an explosion which caused the whole ship to shudder violently. I was conscious of everything in my cabin being thrown about in wild confusion. I rolled out of my bunk and groped for my life-jacket. It was not where I had hung it before turning in. I tried the cabin door, but it would not open. Presumably it had buckled owing to the force of the explosion. Alarm bells were sounding shrilly, and the ship began to heel uncomfortably. I wrenched at the door and finally got it open. I staggered along the steeply canted alley and reached the deck. The ship was now at an angle of about forty-five degrees.

Some of the crew were preparing to lower a boat.

"What happened?" I asked.

"U-boat. Torpedo got us for'ard."

It was a most extraordinary turn of fortune that this of all ships in the convoy – the one that carried the material which might solve the problems of the acoustic torpedo – should herself be torpedoed. We were powerless to do anything to save the sackloads of acoustic parts; these were still in the back of the borrowed staff car, which it was physically impossible to reach among the vehicles on the tank deck. After the combing that Hills and I had made of the site at Houilles, there was nothing to be had back there; we had taken every worthwhile fragment of evidence – I had even persuaded the French to part with their only important discoveries. Now neither we nor the French would be able to reconstruct the acoustic unit of the "Gnat". The means would be lost for ever at the bottom of the Channel. The Germany Navy seemed fated to preserve the secrets of its most deadly torpedo.

But there was one personal loss I could prevent. I called to the men swinging the boat out on the davits ready to lower away: "Wait till I fetch my jacket."

"Be quick about it."

The jacket itself would be most useful to have; the night was bitterly cold. But what I was chiefly concerned to recover was the ring I had bought in Paris for my wife's birthday; it was still in the pocket of my jacket. I went back along the steeply tilting alleyway to the cabin, found the jacket and returned on deck. The boat still had not been lowered. The men were standing by, waiting.

"What is happening?"

"The captain thinks there's still a chance to keep her afloat."

We waited, aware of the stir of activity for'ard. The damage was pretty serious; all the men on the for'ard guns had been killed.

The captain appeared out of the darkness. He said: "I think I can save the ship by filling the starboard ballast tanks and bringing her back on an even keel. The bulkheads seem to be holding abaft the damage area – at least, so far."

Gradually, the angle of the deck became less steep and finally it was back to horizontal. The ship was floating deep in the water, but she was still afloat. Fortunately, the sea was calm.

Another ship closed in on us through the darkness, and a line was passed to the L.S.T. A cable was made fast at our stern, and the other ship steamed cautiously ahead. The cable tautened, and we were under tow, stern first. Speed was out of the question because the L.S.T. had settled so deep in the water that she had become a sluggish, unmanageable thing, a dead weight.

She was also a sitting duck for any U-boat captain looking for an easy kill.

But, miraculously, she was still afloat. We had a reprieve, and if only it lasted long enough we should get our precious sacks of acoustic unit parts ashore. For the rest of the night and all the next day we made our slow, uneasy way. Night came again. It was thirty hours from the time of leaving Le Havre that we made fast alongside the quay at Portland.

There we were faced with the problem of getting our car off the ship. The damage to the fore part of the L.S.T. prevented the lift from the hold working. We explained to the dockyard people our reason for wanting to reach Portsmouth without delay, and they had the car hoisted bodily from the ship. We drove straight to H.M.S. *Vernon*.

The load of bits and pieces which we had brought back set the *Vernon* scientists as difficult a jigsaw puzzle as might be conceived. But, painstakingly, they worked away at their enormous task of sorting out the broken parts and fitting them into place. Gradually, on the benches before them, the outlines of two acoustic units began to take shape. Eventually, both were completed.

But they could not be made to work.

The centre part of the unit consisted of a bakelite tray. The tray contained twelve sockets, in each of which it was clear there should be a valve. The valves formed the vital core of the torpedo control: the amplifier unit. Without them, the unit could not be made to work.

We were still as far from discovering the secrets of the acoustic torpedo as we had been before our dash to Houilles.

As they examined one of the trays, they noticed that there were figures stamped on the bakelite rim of the valve sockets. It seemed fairly certain that these figures were to identify the type of valve which had to go into each particular socket. It looked like the usual German thoroughness, this time to make sure that the assembly workers got the right valve in the right socket. If this were so, it could prove one instance where the Germans had been over-thorough.

At DTMI I told Maitland-Dougall of the problem we had met and of the code numbers we had which might be used to solve the problem, if only we could find someone who knew what type of valves the numbers indicated.

"Your best plan," he said, "is to go to see the Air Force. They have people in their special wireless and radar section who know the classification of every German valve."

I tracked down the department through Air Ministry. The head of the branch agreed to see me at once. I handed him my list and explained why I believed that the numbers on it would identify certain German valves.

"The Navy want to get hold of them urgently, or at least valves like them," I added. "Can you supply me with the British or American equivalents?"

He sent for one of his technical experts and gave him the list, asking him to check if they had the necessary valves in stock. Presently, the expert returned to say that they could supply me with six equivalent valves from their stocks.

"But," he added, "the rest are unknown to us."

"I'm afraid that six won't solve our problem. We must have the full twelve. Have you any idea where the others were made?"

"Offhand, no. But if you'll hang on, I'll see what we can find out."

On his return he said that the valves had probably all been made by the Dutch electrical firm of Philips of Eindhoven.

"But Eindhoven is still in enemy hands," I said. "Isn't there anywhere else we can get them?"

"Just how important is it that you should have these valves?" said the head of the branch.

"I don't think it's putting it too high to say that the whole course of the war at sea may depend on our obtaining them."

"It's like that, is it … ?" The head of the branch paused, his eyes met those of his colleague, and then he said: "Well, we'll have to see what we can do. Leave it with us, will you? I'll get in touch with you as soon as possible."

I returned to the Admiralty to await events. There had been something almost conspiratorial in the manner of the two R.A.F. experts at the end of our conversation. The look that passed between them when I emphasised the importance to the Navy of getting the valves suggested rather more than had the somewhat vague final words of the head of the branch. My guess was that they had something up their sleeves. Even so, I was hardly prepared for the surprise they produced in under twenty-four hours.

The day after I called on them, an R.A.F. officer arrived at our office accompanied by a civilian. The officer introduced himself and said: "I should like you to meet Mr. Van Tromp ..."

I shook hands with the civilian. He was fair-haired and about fifty years of age, tall and with a slight stoop.

The R.A.F. officer explained: "Van Tromp is the managing director of Philips of Eindhoven, who make valves for the Germans."

"You mean that he *was* managing director," I said.

"No, he *is*," said the R.A.F. officer.

"That is so," said Van Tromp gently, smiling at my surprise.

Now that I came to look at him more closely, I could see that his suit had not been tailored in London; there was something peculiarly continental about its cut.

He said: "I heard that the British Navy have found themselves in certain difficulties, and so I have come over to help if I can."

"From Eindhoven?" I asked incredulously.

He nodded. "That is so."

There are times when one desperately wants to ask questions but must not; this was one of them. It would only have embarrassed the R.A.F. officer, because he would not have been able to tell me the methods he had employed to bring Van Tromp to London like this. I had, of course, heard of R.A.F. cloak-and-dagger units which flew Lysander aircraft and flitted about Occupied Europe landing or picking up agents. But this was the first personal contact I had with these operations.

Perhaps the most disconcerting thing about the Dutchman was the casualness with which he dismissed his journey out of enemy-held Holland under the eyes of the Gestapo; he might have stepped off a trolley bus from Hampstead for all the sign he gave that he had been involved in a highly dangerous venture.

His gentle voice, speaking in perfect English, brought me back to his reason for being there: "If you will tell me what your problem is, Commander Lincoln ... ?"

I handed him the list of code numbers for the valves which were required to complete our reconstructed acoustic torpedo unit. He scanned it quickly.

"Ah, yes. We make all of these at Eindhoven. How many do you want?"

"A dozen?" I suggested tentatively, still finding the whole situation a little unreal.

Van Tromp turned to the R.A.F. officer. "If you come in forty-eight hours to the airfield where you picked me up, you can have them."

To me he said: "You shall have twenty sets of these valves – packed for export!"

It came about precisely as he had promised: the German valves manufactured in a factory working under German orders were delivered to me. The acoustic torpedo unit was made to work. At last, our experts were able to discover all they wanted to know about it. And also, of course, this meant that if we wished to manufacture an acoustic torpedo of our own we had the ready-made basis on which to start.

I suspect that the Dutchman's real name was not Van Tromp. All that I was able to learn about him from subsequent inquiries was that he was the leader of an active Resistance group. This possibly explains how the R.A.F. were able to get in touch with him so promptly to bring him to London.

After the liberation, I was briefly in Holland; it was only for a matter of hours owing to the emergency landing of an aircraft in which I was flying to Germany. But I took the opportunity to try to speak to Van Tromp by telephone;

unfortunately, he was not available. I should have liked personally to have thanked him for what he had done. Without his help we possibly should never have ended the quest which began so many years before when, hesitantly, a Cockfosters interrogator came on the telephone to say that a talkative *Feldwebel* had arrived in captivity.

Chapter 14

Across the Rhine

Leave in wartime was always a rather precarious privilege, so when Captain Maitland-Dougall went off in March 1945, to spend a few days at his home in the country, leaving me in charge at DTMI, I hoped nothing would arise to prevent him from enjoying a complete rest from his most exacting duties at the Admiralty. However, before very long a situation developed which cut short his leave abruptly and at the same time involved me in a most unexpected venture. One of the consequences was that, quite fortuitously, a fellow-officer and I became the first British naval officers to cross the Rhine, a distinction which was not entirely appreciated at the time owing to enemy designs on the bridge by which we made the crossing.

There was at the Admiralty a department which went about its duties with a maximum of thoroughness and a complete lack of publicity. What the department was called and how it functioned are matters which do not affect this account. It is only necessary to mention that one afternoon I received a visit from one of its shrewd and efficient officers, who placed some information before me. I could see at once its importance.

The reason my opinion was being asked was that the information contained the letters *SMA*. One of the tasks which I had set myself was to discover the German code letters of every type of underwater weapon, and these had been passed on to the various departments at the Admiralty to whom they might be useful, including that of the officer who had come to see me about this most interesting piece of German supply information.

The *SMA* was a German submarine type of magnetic mine. It was not very difficult to guess why a quantity of these mines were now being sent to Remagen in Rhineland: this was where the American First Army, under General Hodges, had established the first bridgehead across the Rhine.

"This looks," I said, "as if the Germans are getting ready to make a frogman attack with mines on the bridge at Remagen as they did at Nijmegen."

"That was our guess, too," said my visitor. "In that case, we'd better warn the Americans so that they're ready to deal with it."

He went off to arrange this through the Allied Naval Commander, Expeditionary Force – A.N.C.X.F. – and I turned up the recent intelligence summaries dealing with the Allied assault on Germany. On March 7th, the 9th Armoured Division of the U.S. First Army had brilliantly snatched the opportunity to cross the Rhine by the Ludendorff Bridge, which carried the railway over the river at Remagen, when, by some extraordinary circumstance, the Germans had failed to destroy the bridge. A couple of days later, the Americans had captured Erpel, on the other side of the river, and pushed on to Hönnef. They had increased the capacity of the railway bridge by constructing pontoon bridges above and below it, and were rushing men and materials across the river as rapidly as they could. With most of the west bank of the river north of the Moselle now in Allied hands, the Rhine had become the Germans' last barrier against defeat from the west. The American crossing at Remagen was a critical threat which the Germans were desperately doing their utmost to resist. The decision to send mines to Remagen showed their determination to destroy the bridges. If they succeeded, the American troops on the east bank of the Rhine would be in a most unenviable position; they would be cut off from their reinforcements and supplies, and they might be hurled back into the river.

It was clearly imperative that every assistance must be given to the Americans to safeguard their bridges over the Rhine.

As soldiers, the U.S. First Army could hardly be expected to know how to handle sea mines; these were not the sort of weapons with which they would have had occasion to deal. For the same reason, they would be unlikely to know much about the techniques employed by frogmen, for their origins had also been strictly naval.

During my service in the Mediterranean, I had learned a good deal about the methods used by frogmen.

On my way back from Italy, I had called in at Gibraltar to see our DTMI officer there. He was Lieutenant (later Commander) Lionel Crabb. As my friendship with Crabb survived the war, it was a considerable personal shock to me when in 1956 he died suddenly and in mysterious circumstances.

Crabb, who had gone to Gibraltar to train in shallow water diving, was there in the summer of 1942 when underwater damage was suffered by a number of merchant ships. The cause was discovered to be limpet mines which had been attached to ships' bottoms, and Crabb was able to recover a number of these and send them to H.M.S. *Vernon* for examination. When I arrived at Gibraltar, he was still keeping up his dawn routine of diving around ships to see whether there had been any attempts at limpet mine attack, and so I joined forces with him in the work.

At first the explanation of these attacks was thought to be that Italian submarines were approaching Gibraltar at night, as had happened in May, 1941, when three "human torpedoes", each carrying two men, successfully breached the harbour defences. But this view gave way to the belief that enemy agents in Spain were responsible. This turned out to be the true explanation, although the method was rather different from anything that had been suspected by Naval Intelligence. The means chosen by the Italian Navy was highly ingenious and was not revealed until after Italy was out of the war.

Early in the war, an Italian motor vessel of about 5,000 tons, the *Olterra*, sank off the Spanish port of Algeciras across the bay from Gibraltar. The Italian Navy decided to make the

Olterra their base for attack by "human torpedoes" on shipping in Gibraltar harbour. Under the pretext of legitimate salvage operations, they fitted underwater doors in the bows of the vessel behind which were housed their "human torpedoes". The men who rode astride these craft left unseen from Algeciras harbour, crossed the bay and, after placing their explosive charges under vessels moored at Gibraltar, they returned to re-enter the underwater bow doors of the *Olterra*. At any rate, this was what they did when they were successful. Crabb and I went over to Algeciras and examined the *Olterra*. There were still "human torpedoes" in place in the vessel, and from our investigation we were able to learn some valuable information about the techniques employed by enemy frogmen.

This knowledge, combined with long experience studying the workings of German mines, meant that I had much information which might prove useful to the Americans in their efforts to counter attempts to destroy the bridges over the Rhine, should these materialise.

Plainly, it would be utterly inadequate to send them a signal, which would allow no more than a few brief hints to be given. A letter, however long and detailed, would not be very much better; and, furthermore, the Americans would doubtless be so fully occupied with the desperate task of holding the bridgehead and seeking to exploit their advantage in getting troops across the river that they would hardly be expected to appreciate my efforts to supply a correspondence course on a complicated and specialist aspect of naval warfare. As far as I could see, there was only one possible answer. I put through a telephone call to Maitland-Dougall's house in the country.

Since it was an open line, it was inadvisable to go into detail, so all I said was: "I have something very urgent and important I must discuss with you, sir."

"Right, come down as soon as you can, Lincoln."

It was shortly before dinner when I reached his house. He and his wife had Squadron Leader and Mrs. Steele as dinner guests. Steele was from R.A.F. technical intelligence and had worked with us very closely in the past. As he was so much involved in the secrets of our activities, he adjourned with Maitland-Dougall and me to discuss the problem.

"I think the only thing to be done," I said, after explaining the situation, "is for me to leave as soon as possible for Remagen to advise on counter measures."

"I agree," said Maitland-Dougall. "But things are likely to be pretty sticky over there. Do be careful, won't you?"

As always, when any member of his staff was about to undertake a task which might prove dangerous, his concern was for the safety of the person involved. I did not anticipate being too much out of my element in the land fighting on the Rhine, as the experience of the Sicily Campaign and Salerno landing with No. 30 Commando had given me a fair idea of what might be expected. My main concern, in fact, was that our plan would mean that Maitland-Dougall would now have to forego his leave and return to the Admiralty. However, this could not be helped, as he pointed out quickly.

It was agreed that another officer should accompany me, and the choice was Lieutenant A.L. Broom, R.N.V.R., a fellow Devonian who like myself came from Plymouth.

The offer of assistance in dealing with the threat of a frogman attack on the Remagen bridges was accepted by the Americans, and Broom and I received orders from A.N.C.X.F. to proceed at once by air to Paris. On Sunday, March 18th, we took off for Orly.

As we headed across the Channel, I recalled with some amusement that the last time I had flown on this route, during the previous autumn, I had lost a bet. The flight on that occasion had been in the company of Air Chief Marshal Harris, Commander-in-Chief of Bomber Command.

The circumstances leading to it were that shortly beforehand the R.A.F. had bombed a big marshalling yard near Versailles, and when he went over in his own plane to inspect the result "Bomber" Harris had spotted on railway trucks some objects which he took to be aircraft mines. Later he had these photographed by a reconnaissance aircraft, and the pictures, along with his report, came to us at the Admiralty. He asked if an R.M.S.O. could be sent to investigate the objects as soon as possible, and offered to take over the officer personally.

I was assigned for the task and reported to Harris, who was going over to attend a conference at Versailles. With us in the aircraft were Air Marshal Bottomley and Paul Maze, an artist friend of Winston Churchill who had given him painting lessons. Although he had lived many years in England, Maze was French, and the object of his flight was to make a personal report to the Prime Minister on the effect on French sentiment of Allied bombing raids.

During the flight, "Bomber" Harris and I became involved in a discussion on whether the R.A.F. could sink a battleship with bombs. He said they could, I said – rather injudiciously – that they could not. We finished up by having a wager on the issue.

When we landed at Versailles, Maze went off to a nearby village on his quest, and I left for the marshalling yards. It was agreed that we should return to Harris's headquarters at 5.30 p.m. to fly back with him to London.

At the yards, I found that what had looked like mines from the air were in fact large incendiary bomb containers. The trucks were loaded with bombs and a variety of other weapons, none of naval interest. But while I was making the examination, the yards came under heavy German gunfire. This delayed my return, and by the time Maze and I reached Versailles again "Bomber" Harris had already left. He had heard the explosion caused by the shelling and assumed that I had gone up with the "mines"! But later he learned that this had not been so, and he claimed the luncheon I had bet him that a battleship could not be sent to the bottom by bombing. On November 12, 1944, the R.A.F. had sunk the battleship *Tirpitz* in Tromsø Fjord and with it, I fear, my claims to be an aerial strategist.

When Broom and I reached Orly, we were taken to the headquarters in Paris of the A.N.C.X.F., and there we met Colonel Dixon, Chief of Intelligence of the American First

Army. He told us of the arrangements made to get us up to the Rhine, and I learned that as soon as the Americans could dispense with my services I was to go on to the British 21st Army Group, which was commanded by Field-Marshal Montgomery.

The arrangements for our journey up into Germany turned out to be two very small scout planes. The pilot sat in front, the passenger behind. As these were single-engine aircraft, we had to wear parachutes. But I had my Commando pack and a .45 automatic, and there was just not room in the tightly-tailored seat for me, my gear and the parachute. In the end, I had to leave behind a good deal of gear at Orly.

We took off for the airfield at Düren, which stands on the River Roer, twenty or so miles west of Cologne. The two little planes flew companionably close, and Broom and I were able to exchange signals through the domed canopies whenever we spotted anything of interest below. We also kept a wary eye to skyward for any sign of the Luftwaffe; as our aircraft were unarmed our only hope of escape would have been by rapid descent. However, the enemy appeared to have been well routed. During the course of the flight we enjoyed a superb view of the Siegfried Line which seemed to have been taken intact.

On arrival at Düren, it proved impossible to find any airfield in serviceable condition, owing to the heavy bombing and shelling which the area had experienced, and we were forced to return to Eschweiler. Here we ran into difficulties. The airfield authorities obviously regarded us as strongly suspect, and they could not be blamed for harbouring doubts about us. After all, for a couple of strangers to arrive unannounced so close on the heels of the retreating enemy, for them to be dressed in khaki battle-dress bearing a combination of naval and Commando badges and then to declare themselves as British naval officers on their way to join the U.S. First Army must have sounded highly improbable. Eventually we were found by an officer from the First Army, who had been sent to meet us, and we were then driven to Remagen.

General Hodges wanted to see me as soon as I arrived. He had his headquarters at a village near the Rhine. A short and stocky man, tough and determined, he gave the impression of being a first-class soldier. He wanted to know what my experience was in dealing with frogmen, and I told him of what I had learned in the Mediterranean.

"Well, Commander," he said, "I want to thank you for coming. I much appreciate the fact that the British Navy have sent you. We've taken some steps already, which you'll be told about, and I'll give orders that you're to have a free hand."

After discussions with the Chief of Intelligence, the Chief Engineer and the officer responsible for troop movements, I went down to the Rhine to decide what might be done to improve defences. There had been an attempt by frogmen the previous night to destroy the Kripp-Linz pontoon bridge, and some damage had been done but nothing very serious. Two frogmen, one in a dying condition, had been captured, and the hunt was on for others who were thought to have tried to escape into the woods by the river. The warning sent by the Admiralty had fully alerted the Americans to the danger of attack by frogmen, and they had fixed a boom across the river. As a result of the overnight attack, they had now put a second log boom into position.

There was no doubting the German determination at all costs to destroy the bridges. Even as we surveyed the scene, Luftwaffe bombers and fighters thundered in to attack. The anti-aircraft barrage drove off the aircraft leaving the two pontoon crossings still intact. As I later reported to the Admiralty: "The ack-ack fire surrounding the bridges was the heaviest concentration that I had ever seen."

The centre span of the railway bridge, linking the two wooded banks of the Rhine, had already gone. But it had required enormous effort by the Germans to achieve this; in addition to ordinary heavy artillery shelling, they had used a 240mm railway gun – the type from which we had suffered on the Normandy beach-head at "Juno" Area – V-2 rockets and the attacking force of nearly four hundred aircraft.

Their failure to destroy the Rhine crossings by artillery and air attack seemed to make it still more certain that, despite the previous abortive attempt, the frogmen would be ordered to make an all-out effort to get their mines in position. Even if they managed to explode one of the mines against either of those frail pontoon bridges, the effect would be disastrous. I decided that the only safe course was to make sure they were stopped long before they reached the bridges.

With this in mind, I made these suggestions to the American officers responsible:

Tank searchlights should be arranged some 1,000 yards upstream of each bridge so as to give a continuous lighted area for some four hundred yards. Below this area of concentrated illumination, other tank searchlights should be placed – fortunately, the Americans were lavishly equipped – and these should be switched on at brief intervals. The idea was that when the frogmen came to the fully lit area they would have to submerge – or perish. As soon as they reached the darkened stretch of water they would surface again. But this would never be left dark long enough to allow them through. In the sudden blaze of light where they had expected the comforting darkness they would be seen.

A boat patrol should operate in the area above the bridges, dropping ten pound high explosive charges every five minutes. Even if these explosions did not jar the frogmen into insensibility, they would cause sufficient underwater disturbance to have a highly demoralising effect.

The Americans had been banking on heavy calibre guns for use against the swimmers, but I did not consider these possessed a quick enough rate of fire; I suggested 40mm Bofors guns instead.

And, against floating mines, I suggested that .50 calibre machine guns should be used.

I also pointed out that it was unwise to neglect the possibility of an attack upstream by such means as explosive motor boats, and suggested that 40mm guns were the best defence against these.

All these measures were put into effect.

The frogmen would enter the water at some point upstream on the east bank which was still in German possession. As the whole west bank was now in Allied hands, the swimmers could be expected to give that as wide a berth as possible. The chances were that they would be more likely to be spotted from the east bank. I decided that Broom and I should make our headquarters there.

A young American lieutenant arrived with an armoured car to take us across. He was a slim-built youngster and not more than twenty-one. From his hairstyle, which was a precursor of the crew-cut, he might have been a German. He was in fact a German American, and he spoke German fluently.

We climbed aboard the armoured car and set off across the Rhine by one of the pontoon bridges. Once we were on the far side we knew that our prospects of return depended entirely on the success of the plans made to forestall the frogmen. If even a couple of them were to get through and destroy the pontoon bridges, our line of retreat would be cut off. We should have to take our chances with the troops. But our young American lieutenant proceeded to show that the military were able to look after themselves and us, at least as far as our immediate needs were concerned.

We drove to a village, and the American sent for the local burgomaster. He told the German that we should require good accommodation for the night. The burgomaster returned after a short while to say that he had found a comfortable house where we should be welcome.

"The people are not Nazis," he assured us, rather piously, I thought.

We went along to the house. The matronly *hausfrau*, who had put on her finest white apron to receive us, assured us that she had placed her best bedroom at our disposal. She apologised for the fact that we should have to use oil lamps, but owing to the battle in progress the electricity supply for the whole area had failed. Actually, considering the quantity of high explosive that both sides were using, it was surprising that the area had survived with so little serious damage.

I sent Broom up to investigate the room to make sure that it was satisfactory. When he came down a few moments later, he looked thoroughly indignant.

"She's sabotaged the bed!" he said.

I went up expecting to find at least a bomb under the pillow, but as soon as I saw the bed I realised that, far from being guilty of sabotage, our hostess had put herself out to make us comfortable. She had laid a *Federbet* on top of the blankets to make sure we should be warm. As this German version of the eiderdown looked like an enormous mattress, Broom had assumed she had turned the bed upside down as a blow for the Fatherland.

"Now we've got the accommodation fixed," said our American guide, "let's get to the local gauleiter's home as quickly as possible."

"What for?" I asked innocently.

"If we get there before anyone else," he said, "we'll find the best brandy and cigars in the neighbourhood."

For such a very young man he seemed quickly to have acquired the instincts of a seasoned campaigner.

The obliging burgomaster showed the way. The supplies we found at the house suggested the gauleiter was a man who enjoyed good living.

I questioned the legality of this foraging. The American, who was enjoying himself hugely, gave the official ruling.

"We must not loot," he said. "But we can liberate."

I liked his expression; we proceeded to liberate.

When night fell, fortified by the gauleiter's brandy and soothed by his cigars, we began our vigil. This is what I said in my report to the Admiralty at the time:

> During the two nights spent in this bridgehead, during which we were able to cross the Rhine on the pontoon bridges, we surveyed all the defences up and down river, including the individual searchlights by various booms,

altering the siting of lights and guns so as to avoid giving the swimmers protected areas under the steep bank on the eastern shore.

The beams of tank searchlights brilliantly illuminated the surface of the river. The current swirled swiftly under the powerful beams. It would be impossible for anything to break surface without detection. And it would require exceptional courage and determination on the part of German frogmen – *Kampfschwimmer*, as the enemy called them – to attempt to get past the blindingly bright areas kept permanently under searchlight beams. Yet I did not doubt that there were men sufficiently fanatical to attempt it.

They came, swimming miles down the dark, cold waters of the Rhine. They had only their rubber suits to protect them against the icy cold water, and only their physical endurance to fight the hazards of the swift-rushing current. At the end of their long swim they must have realised, when they saw ahead the dazzling intensity of the massed searchlights, that their chances of success were infinitesimal. But still they came.

My account to the Admiralty stated:

> I am pleased to be able to report that of the three attempts made by swimmers on those pontoon bridges all attempts were defeated by blowing the swimmers out of the water before they could reach their objective. In the first attempt the swimmers had apparently reached to within a hundred yards of the Kripp-Linz bridge, but the second and third attempts were defeated in the lighted area about a thousand yards upstream.

In view of the contribution Broom and I had been able to make, I could now feel less guilty about Maitland-Dougall's recall to the Admiralty; it did not seem that his leave had been unwarrantably curtailed.

It was now time for me to report to the 21st Army Group. But before doing so I instructed the bomb disposal officers of the American First Army in the rendering safe procedure for *GS*, *GN*, and *GL* mines, and in the methods of dealing with explosive motor boats and "human torpedoes". General Kean, Chief-of-Staff to General Hodges, asked me to leave behind Lieutenant Broom with the bridge guards at Kripp, and I agreed to this. Later Broom found himself in Brussels, where it fell to him to render safe no less than a hundred aircraft mines which the Germans had left at the airfield of Melsbroek. For this he received the George Medal.

*

On the afternoon of March 20th, I flew to Brussels, to the headquarters of the 21st Army Group. There I reported to Brigadier Williams who was in charge of intelligence services, and he asked me to leave early next morning for Venlo, just over the German frontier, a drive of about four hours. At Venlo the British Second Army Main Headquarters were situated; it was there also that Field-Marshal Montgomery had taken the famous caravan from which he conducted his battles.

My arrival was reported to Monty, and back came the instruction: "Acquaint yourself with the assault plan for the crossing of the Rhine."

As Colonel Murphy, who was in charge of intelligence, explained to me the details of the operation planned, I realised that I had arrived at a moment of history. Monty had three armies under his command – the Second British, the First Canadian and the Ninth U.S. The crossings planned were due to take place in little over forty-eight hours' time. It was to be an enterprise of breath-taking magnitude. The centre point of the effort was to be Wesel, but crossings were to extend some miles upstream and downstream of the town. Preparations had been on a prodigious scale. While the American crossing at Remagen had been a matter of snatching at a chance opportunity, there was to be no element of chance in Monty's crossing. Months of meticulous planning had gone into the operation, massive quantities of material had been assembled; for a fortnight hundreds of bombing aircraft had deluged West

Germany with thousands of tons of bombs. This was a project based on sheer military efficiency and methodical thoroughness. Murphy pointed out the positions on the map where it was intended the assault forces should cross and where it was intended ultimately to have pontoon bridges.

"This," he said, "is where you come in."

I was introduced to Brigadier Parham to discuss plans for the defence of the assault craft and bridges against underwater or waterborne attacking forces. All that day and the whole of the next were spent in conferences, much of the time with officers of the 100th Anti-Aircraft Brigade under Brigadier Turner, who had the responsibility for defending the bridges.

There was only one point in all the discussions over which there was not immediate agreement. The army wanted to put the assault craft into the water something like two hours before they were due to make the crossings. This seemed to me to be exposing the craft to considerable danger from underwater attacks. I thought the longest they should risk was quarter of an hour. So strenuously did I argue this that the matter was put up to Monty for his decision. He agreed that the shorter the time the assault craft were in the water before the crossing the better.

On my arrival at Parham's headquarters there occurred the first of three unexpected encounters. One of his staff officers was a Captain Hyde. As soon as I saw him, I recognised him as one of two brothers who had been in my college at Oxford. His brother was in the R.A.F., and by chance I had met him the year before in Malta.

Next, when it was time for me to leave the headquarters and to go on to an intelligence centre for final discussions, an officer was called over to escort me – the village was under heavy shellfire at the time. The escort proved to be Major Ashworth, whom I had known as a barrister before the war. (He is now Mr. Justice Ashworth.)

Finally, just before I went down to the Rhine on the night before the assault, I had to visit some forward intelligence officers at a coal-mining village close to the river. One of the officers was named Amswych, and though I had not met him before he proved to be the son of a man who had been a great friend of mine for years, Captain Amswych, who had served with distinction in the First World War.

As a naval officer, I had hardly anticipated that in a matter of a few hours the army would supply so many links with my past.

It had been decided that after having completed my advice to the British Second Army I should proceed up river to the American Ninth Army under the command of General Simpson who were considered to have the most exposed flank from the point of view of river attack. On the evening of March 22nd, I arrived at the 16th Corps of the Ninth Army. Here again a series of discussions ensued, and all lights, light artillery and heavy machine guns, booms and other protective equipment were more or less put at my disposal. I was asked to suggest how these could best be sited in relation to the bridges, which were to be flung across the Rhine. To cover the period between the building of the bridges and the completion of protective booms, I suggested boat patrols should operate to drop ten pound explosive charges throughout the night.

"And what do we do about floating mines being used against assault craft as well as the bridges?" asked the 16th Corps commander.

"The only thing to do," I said, "is to keep a careful look-out and try to destroy any floating mines by small arms and heavy calibre machine gun fire. I should suggest also that to minimise the risk you do not put your assault craft into the water until the last possible moment."

This was agreed.

On the evening of Friday, March 23rd, everything had been prepared for the assault. I joined Colonel Deery of the Tank Destroyer Section to go to the extreme right flank of the Allied assault, which would move over the river from a point about two hundred yards north of the township of Orsoy. If there were to be any attempt by *Kampfschwimmer* forces, this was the most likely place of attack.

We drove towards the riverside in an open jeep. I was seated in the back. American infantrymen were moving up in widespread formation. As we crawled along in the jeep, a young American plodded stolidly behind us. On his face was all the apprehension of a man who was going into action for the first time.

"Don't worry about it," I said, trying to cheer him up. "I've been through it at Sicily and Salerno. It's not as bad as it sounds."

But the youngster's face remained as glum as ever.

"Here," I said, pulling out a tin of hard candy the Americans had given me, "have some candy."

"No, sir," he gulped. "I couldn't eat a thing."

The jeep pulled ahead. I never saw him again. I hope that he did not find it as bad as he anticipated it would be.

To the north the British barrage had already started, and from the position we took on the dyke by the riverside it was possible to see almost the whole of the assault area. The main barrage of the American forces was not due to begin until 2 a.m. next day, and we spent an hour in surveying the defences along the river bank which were intended to deal with the double menace of infiltrating enemy patrols, floating mines and saboteurs. There was a certain amount of desultory firing going on in this sector from both sides, and the heavy American artillery was being answered by occasional mortar shells.

As the enemy were only three hundred yards away across the river, we had to carry out all conversation as quietly as possible, and we had to be careful to avoid being outlined against the sky when crossing the dyke to the shore of the river where the assault craft were waiting in readiness for the order to launch.

About midnight a shell fell so close to our jeep that Deery and I had to throw ourselves bodily into a foxhole in the side of the dyke. There we stayed, about a hundred yards from the assault craft, looking out on the river which was by now partially illuminated by searchlights. At 2 a.m. the American barrage began in earnest, and the Germans replied with heavy mortar fire which began to fall along the top of the dyke behind us. This caused some casualties among the tank destroyer crews along the embankment, and one gun was put completely out of action by a direct hit.

As the enemy appeared to have the accurate range of the dyke, we deemed it wiser, after a short while, to move back as quickly as possible, between salvoes, to an artillery observation post in a house just behind the dyke. From there we could maintain our watch on the river and keep in touch with the assault parties by telephone if necessary.

Monty had placed his artillery in three lines, practically wheel to wheel, for a distance of something like seventeen miles. The effect of the barrage was cataclysmal.

In the account written at the time, this is how I saw it:

> The whole spectacle throughout the night was completely awe-inspiring, the effect of the immense bombardment being clearly visible along the whole front. The German shore at times became a complete mass of flame, and the effect was heightened when the seventeen-pounders on the very shores of the river opened up at point blank range against the opposite dykes, only 1,100 feet across the river. Finally, just before the assault, .50 calibre machine guns poured ribbons of tracer into the opposite beaches. Then a heavy smoke-screen blotted out the river as the assault craft pushed off.

The leading assault craft safely crossed, and soon a regular ferry was in operation. The American barrage was shifted to the south towards the direction of Alten and Duisburg Ruhrort. Deery and I decided to get back to Corps headquarters to learn how the assault as a whole was going. Enemy shelling continued, and now it included air bursts. We had to run the gauntlet to reach the end of the nearby village. Ultimately, at about 5.30 a.m., we reached Corps Headquarters. There the reports were all of success.

Three hours later, with the engineer colonel, I went up river to the site where a pontoon bridge was being built at Wallach.

The engineers were wasting no time; some idea of the difficulty they faced with such early bridging was shown by the fact that as they began to get their pontoons into position, a German machine gun in a wood close to the opposite bank opened fire on them. The artillery was called up, and soon this opposition was silenced. By evening the pontoon bridge spanned the river and was open to traffic. One of the three log booms, which had been prepared and laid along the beach in readiness, had been swung into position above the bridge as protection against attack by frogmen. At my suggestion, the booms had been wound with barbed wire to make them a still more formidable barrier.

At 9.30 p.m. I was called to the telephone. A Second Army intelligence officer was on the line.

He said: "I want to warn you of the possibility of an attack by explosive motor boats from the direction of Wesel."

The American engineers and I consulted the maps and decided that the attack, if it came, would be most likely from either the Lippe Canal or the Lippe River. Searchlights and Bofors guns were moved downstream of the bridge in readiness, and all troops were alerted. However, no attack materialised from this quarter or with this weapon.

But that night from the Lippe River an attack with floating mines was launched on the partially completed British bridges farther downstream. Brigadier Turner's Artillery Brigade went into action. All the mines were exploded by heavy calibre machine gun fire before they could reach the bridges.

By Sunday, March 25th, I was satisfied that all possible precautions against enemy attempts at interference with the bridges had been taken along the whole of the front of the 21st Army Group, and so I took leave of the army and returned to London by way of Paris. On the morning of March 27th, I was back at my desk in the Admiralty.

From the intelligence reports that were coming in it was perfectly obvious that during the week spent with the British and American armies I had seen the delivery of what was to prove the death blow to Germany on the Western Front.

Index